6,000
Most-Used
CENTURY 21®
Shorthand
Outlines

EDWARD L. CHRISTENSEN, Ph.D.

Professor of Business Management
Brigham Young University

DEVERN J. PERRY, Ed.D.

Associate Professor of
Business Education
Brigham Young University

Shorthand Plates Written by
STANFORD D. E

D1520229

Published by

R15 SOUTH-WESTERN PUBLISHING CO.

CINCINNATI   WEST CHICAGO, ILL.   DALLAS   PELHAM MANOR, N.Y.
PALO ALTO, CALIF.   BRIGHTON, ENGLAND

A
B
C
D
E
F
G
H
I
J
K
L
M
N
O
P
Q
R
S
T
U
V
W
X-Y
Z

ISBN: 0-538-18150-8

Library of Congress Catalog Card Number: 72-90734

   3 4 5 6 7 K 0 9 8 7 6 5

Printed in the United States of America

PREFACE

The book 6,000 MOST-USED SHORTHAND OUT-LINES is designed as a ready-reference for you as you develop your skill with CENTURY 21 Shorthand. The words, phrases, and special outlines you will need as your skill progresses and as you use shorthand in office work are presented in alphabetic order for ease of location.

Exactly 5,170 of the most-used words were selected through computer analysis for this book together with their shorthand outlines. *These words account for over 96 percent of the words you will write in shorthand dictation.* If you know these outlines, you will construct less than 4 percent of what you write as "new" words!

The 175 CENTURY 21 Speedforms are included in this book. Words selected as Speedforms were carefully analyzed before inclusion. As a result, the 500 most-used words are easy to write in their original CENTURY 21 form or as facile Speedforms. About 57 percent of the Speedforms appear in the first 500 frequently used words, and *these 500 words account for 72 percent of business or general vocabulary!*

Moreover, the Speedforms and Speedform-related words (e.g., *delivery, delivering,* and *delivered* are related to the Speedform: *deliver)* account for one *out of every seven* words appearing in your ready-reference book, the 6,000 MOST-USED SHORT-HAND OUTLINES.

The 100 common phrases have also been selected—on the basis of frequency and facility—to be included in the 6,000 MOST-USED SHORTHAND OUT-LINES. If the 100 commonly used phrases are used automatically by the shorthand writer, they will be an aid in speed development. However, if you hesitate to recall whether or not a group of words should be phrased (written together), speed is actually lost.

This common-phrase list contains but a small part of all the possible combinations of words in CENTURY 21 Shorthand. In fact, advanced texts in this system present and apply hundreds of feasible CENTURY 21 phrases. However, *the 100 commonly used phrases are powerful* and they should be available in a special list of phrases to be fully mastered.

A number of other shorthand lists which contain special abbreviations and pertinent terms, along with shorthand outlines, are contained in 6,000 MOST-USED SHORTHAND OUTLINES. These frequently used special reference lists, which are of value to the beginning shorthand student as well as the capable stenographer, include the following:

Beginning on page 137, the 5,170 most-used words are listed in the order of the frequency of their use, in 100-word groups. This specially arranged list indicates the relative importance of each 100-word group in reading and writing shorthand.

Your 6,000 MOST-USED SHORTHAND OUTLINES is an excellent ready-reference support to you in accomplishing a high level of shorthand competency in the classroom as well as an efficient performance on the job.

1. *Days of the week* . . . based upon the sounds of the official abbreviations.

2. *Months of the year* . . . based upon the common abbreviation of each month, with the short names — *May*, *June*, and *July* — written in full.

3. *Common Surnames* . . . based upon a frequency study entitled "America's 216 Most Common Surnames."

4. *Frequent abbreviations* . . . based upon common commercial abbreviations such as writing of quantities, fractions, dollar amounts, and highly frequent abbreviations (e.g., *f.o.b.* and *U.S.*).

5. *Correspondence outlines* . . . based upon three lists of highly frequent correspondence data: common salutations, complimentary closings, and other correspondence elements.

6. *Recommended state abbreviations* . . . based upon the U.S. Postal Service two-letter ZIP Code designations for the fifty states as well as other geographic abbreviations.

7. *Ranally Metro Areas in the U.S.* . . . based upon the 211 largest city areas as published in the *1972 Commercial Atlas & Marketing Guide*.

8. *Largest Metropolitan Areas and Cities of the World* . . . based upon the 50 largest city areas of the world as published in the *1972 Commercial Atlas & Marketing Guide*.

Edward L. Christensen

Devern J. Perry

TABLE OF CONTENTS

LEGEND

a. adjective

CF Contracted/Correspondence form

n. noun

SF Speedform

SFR Speedform related word

v. verb

A

a SF	
abandoned	
abandonment	
abilities	
ability	
able SF	
about SF	
above	
abroad	
absence	
absolute	
absolutely	
abstract	
academic	
academy	
accept SF	
acceptable SFR	
acceptance SFR	
accepted SFR	
accepting SFR	
access	

accessories	
accessory	
accident	
accidental	
accidents	
accommodate	
accommodations	
accompanied SFR	
accompany SFR	
accompanying SFR	
accomplish	
accomplished	
accomplishment	
accomplishments	
accord SF	
accordance SFR	
according SFR	
accordingly SFR	
account SFR	
accountants SFR	
accounting SFR	
accounts SFR	
accrual	
accrued	

accumulate		acted		
accumulated		acting		
accuracy		action		
accurate		actions		
accurately		active	SF	
achieve		actively	SFR	
achieved		activities	SFR	
achievement		activity	SF	
achievements		acts		
acknowledge		actual		
acknowledged		actually		
acknowledgment		acute		
acquaint		ad		
acquaintance		add		
acquainted		added		
acquire		adding		
acquired		addition		
acquiring		additional		
acquisition		additionally		
acre		additions		
acreage		address		
acres		addressed		
across		addresses		
act		addressing		

adds		ad valorem	
adequate		advance SF	
adequately		advanced SFR	
adjacent		advancement SFR	
adjust SFR		advances SFR	
adjusted SFR		advantage SF	
adjuster SFR		advantages SFR	
adjusters SFR		adverse	
adjusting SFR		advertise SF	
adjustment SFR		advertised SFR	
adjustments SFR		advertisement SFR	
administered SFR		advertising SFR	
administration SFR		advice SF	
administrative SFR		advisable SFR	
administrator SFR		advise SF	
administrators SFR		advised SFR	
admission		adviser SFR	
admitted		advises SFR	
adolescents		advising SFR	
adopt		advisory SFR	
adopted		affairs	
adoption		affect SF	
ads		affected SFR	
adult		affecting SFR	

affiliated		agreements	
affiliation		agrees	
afford		agricultural SFR	
afforded		agriculture SF	
affords		ahead	
afraid		aid	
after SF		aids	
afternoon SFR		aim	
afternoons SFR		aims	
again		air	
against		aircraft	
age		airlines	
agencies		airmail	
agency		airport	
agent		airways	
agents		album	
ages		albums	
aggregate		alcoholic	
aggressive		alert	
ago		alive	
agree		all	
agreeable		alleviate	
agreed		allied	
agreement		allocated	

allocation		amended	
allow		amendment	
allowable		amendments	
allowance		ammunition	
allowances		among	
allowed		amortized	
allowing		amount SF	
allows		amounting SFR	
almost		amounts SFR	
alone		ample	
along		an SF	
already		analysis	
also		analyze	
alter		analyzed	
alternate a., n.; v.		and SF	
alternative		angle	
alternatives		animal	
although		anniversary	
aluminum		announce SF	
always		announced SFR	
am SF		announcement SFR	
amateur		announcements SFR	
amazing		announcing SFR	
ambulance		annual	

annually		apology	
annuities		apparel	
annuity		apparent	
annum		apparently	
another		appeal	
answer		appeals	
answered		appear	
answering		appearance	
answers		appeared	
anticipate		appearing	
anticipated		appears	
antitrust		appendix	
anxious SF		appliance	
any SF		appliances	
anybody SFR		applicable	
anyone SFR		applicant	
anything SFR		applicants	
anytime SFR		application	
anyway SFR		applications	
anywhere SFR		applied	
apartment SFR		applies	
apartments SFR		apply	
apologies		applying	
apologize		appoint	

appointed		area	
appointment		areas	
appointments		aren't SFR	
apportionment		argument	
appraisal		arguments	
appraised		arise	
appreciate SF		arises	
appreciated SFR		arising	
appreciation SFR		arm	
appreciative SFR		armed	
approach		arms	
approaching		army	
appropriate a., v.		around	
appropriation		arrange	
approval		arranged	
approve		arrangement	
approved		arrangements	
approximate SF		arranging	
approximately SFR		arrears	
aptitude		arrival	
architect CF		arrive	
architects CF		arrived	
architectural CF		arrives	
are SF		arriving	

Word	Outline	Word	Outline
art		assignments	
article		assist	
articles		assistance	
artists		assistant	
arts		assistants	
as SF		assisting	
aside		associate SF	
ask		associated SFR	
asked		associates SFR	
asking		association SFR	
aspect		associations SFR	
aspects		assortment	
assemble		assume	
assembled		assumed	
assemblies		assuming	
assembling		assumption	
assembly		assurance SFR	
assessed		assure SFR	
assessments		assured SFR	
asset		assures SFR	
assets		assuring SFR	
assign		asthma	
assigned		at SF	
assignment		atmosphere	

attach		authoritative	
attached		authorities	
attaching		authority	
attachment		authorization	
attachments		authorize	
attack		authorized	
attempt		authorizing	
attempted		auto	
attempting		automatic	
attempts		automatically	
attend		automobile	
attendance		automobiles	
attended		automotive	
attending		auxiliary	
attention SF		avail	
attitude		availability	
attorney		available	
attorneys		avenue	
attractive		average	
audience		averaged	
audit		averages	
auditor		aviation	
auditorium		avoid	
author		avoided	

await	balances
awaiting	bales
award	ball
awarded	ballot
awards	band
aware	bank
away	banker
axle	bankers
	banking
B	banks
	banner
baby	banquet
baby's	bar
back	bargain
backed	bargaining
background SFR	barrels
backing	bars
backs	base
bad	based
badly	basic
bag	basically
bags	basin
balance	basis
balanced	bath

battery	before
bay	began
be SF	begin
beach	beginning
beans	begins
bear	begun
bearing	behalf
bearings	behind
beautiful	being SFR
beautifully	belief
beauty	believe
beaver	believed
became	believes
because	bell
become	below
becomes	belt
becoming	beneficial
bed	beneficiaries
bedroom	beneficiary
bedrooms	benefit
beds	benefits
beef	bequest
been SF	bequests
beetles	besides

best		bit	
better		black	
between		blank	
beverages		blanket	
beyond		blankets	
bid		blanks	
bidder		bless	
bidders		blind	
bids		block	
big		blocks	
bigger		blood	
biggest		blotters	
bill		blue	
billed		board	
billet		boards	
billing		boat	
billion		boats	
bills		body	
binder		bond	
binders		bonding	
binding		bonds	
birds		bone	
birth		bonus	
birthday		bonuses	

book		bracket	
bookkeeping		branch	
booklet		branches	
booklets		brand	
books		brands	
boom		brass	
boost		break	
booth		breakdown	SFR
born		breaker	
borrow		breakfast	
borrowed		breaking	
borrowing		brick	
both		bridge	
bottle		bridges	
bottles		brief	
bottom		briefly	
bought		bright	
boulevard		bring	
bound		bringing	
boundaries		brings	
box		broad	
boxes		broadcast	
boy		broader	
boys		brochure	SFR

brochures SFR		
broken		
broker		
brokerage		
brokers		
brother		
brothers		
brought		
brown		
brush		
brushes		
budget		
buff		
build		
builder		
builders		
building		
buildings		
built		
bulk		
bulletin		
bulletins		
burden		
bureau		

bureaus	
burner	
bus	
bushels	
business SF	
businesses SFR	
businessman SFR	
businessmen SFR	
busy	
but	
butter	
button	
buy	
buyer	
buyers	
buying	
buys	
by SF	
bylaws	

C

cabinet	
cabinets	

cable		cane	
calcium		canned SFR	
calculating		cannot SFR	
calculator		cans SFR	
calendar		can't SFR	
call		cap	
called		capabilities	
calling		capable	
calls		capacity	
came		capital	
camera		capitol	
camp		captain	
campaign		captioned	
campaigns		car	
campus		carbon	
can SF		carbons	
cancel		card	
canceled		cards	
canceling		care	
cancellation		career	
cancer		careers	
candidate		careful	
candidates		carefully	
candy		cargo	

C

Word	Shorthand	Word	Shorthand
carload		category	
carpet		caterpillar	
carried		cattle	
carrier		caught	
carriers		cause	
carries		caused	
carry		causes	
carrying		causing	
cars		cease	
carton		cedar	
cartons		ceiling	
case		celebration	
cases		cement	
cash		cent	
cashier		center	
cashiers		centers	
casing		central	
cast		cents	
casualty		century	
catalog		certain	
catalogs		certainly	
catastrophe		certificate	SF
catch		certificates	SFR
categories		certification	SFR

certified	SFR	charges	
certify	SF	charitable	
chain		charity	
chair		chart	
chairman	SF	charter	
chairs		charts	
challenge		chattel	
challenges		cheaper	
challenging		check	
chamber		checked	
chambers		checking	
chance		checks	
chances		cheese	
change	SF	chemical	
changed	SFR	chemicals	
changes	SFR	chemistry	
changing	SFR	chest	
channel		chief	
chapel		child	
chapter		children	
character		children's	
characteristics	CF	child's	
charge		chocolate	
charged		choice	

choose		claims	
choosing		clarification	
chosen		clarify	
church		class	
churches		classes	
circle		classification	
circuit		classifications	
circuits		classroom	
circular		clause	
circulars		clay	
circulating		clean	
circulation		cleaned	
circumstances	CF	cleaner	
cite		cleaning	
cities		clear	
citizen		clearance	
citizens		cleared	
citrus		clearing	
city		clearly	
civic		clerical	
civil		clerk	
civilian		clerks	
claim		client	
claimed		clients	

clinic		coded	
clinical		coding	
clinics		coffee	
close		cold	
closed		collateral	
closely		colleagues	
closer		collect	
closes		collected	
closest		collecting	
closing		collection	
cloth		collections	
clothes		collectors	
clothing		college	
club		colleges	
clubs		color	
coach		colored	
coal		colorful	
coast		colors	
coat		column	
coated		columns	
coating		combination	
coatings		combine	
coats		combined	
code		come	

comes		commodities	
comfort		commodity	
comfortable		common	
coming		commonly	
commander		commonwealth	
commanding		communicate	
commence		communication	
commencement		communications	
commencing		communism	
commend		communist	
commensurate		communities	
comment		community	
comments		companies SFR	
commerce		companion	
commercial		company SF	
commission		comparable	
commissioner		compare	
commissioners		compared	
commissions		comparing	
commitment		comparison	
commitments		compensation	
committed		compete	
committee SF		competent	
committees SFR		competing	

Word	Shorthand	Word	Shorthand
competition		comptroller SFR	
competitive		computed	
competitors		computer	
compilation		computing	
compiled		concept	
complaint		concepts	
complaints		concern	
complete		concerned	
completed		concerning	
completely		concerns	
completing		concise	
completion		conclude	
complex		concluded	
compliance		conclusion	
complicated		conclusions	
compliment		conclusive	
complimentary		concrete	
compliments		condensed	
comply		condition SF	
components		conditioned SFR	
composed		conditioning SFR	
comprehensive		conditions SFR	
compressor		conduct	
compressors		conducted	

conducting	connection
conference	connections
conferences	conscientious
confidence	consent
confident	consequently
confidential	conservation SFR
confined	conservative SFR
confirm	consider SF
confirmation	considerable SFR
confirming	considerably SFR
conflict	consideration SFR
conform SFR	considerations SFR
confronted	considered SFR
confused	considering SFR
confusing	consignee
confusion	consist
congratulate	consistent
congratulations	consistently
congress	consisting
congressional	consists
congressman	consolidated
congressmen	constant
conjunction CF	constantly
connected	constitute

constitutes		containing	SFR	
constitution		contains	SFR	
constitutional		contemplate		
construct	SF	contemplated		
constructed	SFR	contemplating		
constructing	SFR	content		
construction	SFR	contents		
constructive	SFR	contest		
consult		contests		
consultant		contingent		
consultation		continually		
consulting		continuation		
consumer		continue		
consumers		continued		
consuming		continues		
consumption		continuing		
contact	SF	continuous		
contacted	SFR	continuously		
contacting	SFR	contract	SF	
contacts	SFR	contracting	SFR	
contain	SF	contractor	SFR	
contained	SFR	contractors	SFR	
container	SFR	contracts	SFR	
containers	SFR	contrary		

contribute	SF	
contributed	SFR	
contributing	SFR	
contribution	SFR	
contributions	SFR	
control	SF	
controlled	SFR	
controllers	SFR	
controls	SFR	
convenience	SF	
convenient	SF	
conveniently	SFR	
convention	SF	
conventions	SFR	
conversation		
conversations		
conversion		
convert		
converted		
convertible		
convey		
conviction		
convince		
convinced		

cook	
cool	
co-op	
cooperate	
cooperating	
cooperation	
cooperative	
cooperatives	
coordinated	
coordinating	
coordination	
copies	
copper	
copy	
copying	
cordial	
cordially	CF
core	
corn	
corner	
corporate	
corporation	
corporations	
corps	

correct		count	SF	
corrected		counter	SFR	
correcting		counties	SFR	
correction		countries		
corrections		country		
correctly		county	SFR	
correspondence	SF	couple		
correspondent	SFR	coupon		
corresponding	SFR	coupons		
corrosion		courage		
corrugated		course		
cost		courses		
costing		court		
costly		courtesies		
costs		courtesy		
cottage		courts		
cotton		cover		
could		coverage		
couldn't		coverages		
council		covered		
counsel		covering		
counseling		covers		
counselor		cream		
counselors		create		

created		curriculum		
creates		custom	SF	
creating		customary	SFR	
creative		customer	SFR	
credentials		customers	SFR	
credit		cut		
credited		cuts		
credits		cutting		
creek		cycle		
crew		cylinder		
criminal				
critical				
criticism				

D

crop	dailies
crops	daily
cross	dairy
crude	dam
cubic	damage
cultural	damaged
cure	damages
currencies	damaging
currency	dance
current	danger
currently	dangerous

D

dangers		decided	
data		decision	
date		decisions	
dated		declared	
dates		decline	
daughter		declined	
daughters		decrease	
day		decreased	
days		dedicated	
dead		dedication	
deadline		deduct	
deal		deducted	
dealer		deductible	
dealers		deduction	
dealing		deductions	
deals		deed	
dean		deem	
deans		deemed	
death		deep	
debit		deeply	
debt		defective	
debts		defendant	
deceased		defense	
decide		defer	

deferred		democracy		
deficit		democratic		
defined		demonstrate	CF	
definite		demonstrated	CF	
definitely		demonstration	CF	
definition		denominations		
degree		dental		
degrees		department	SF	
delay		departments	SFR	
delayed		departure		
delaying		depend		
delays		dependable		
delegates		dependent		
delighted		dependents		
delinquent	CF	depending		
deliver	SF	depends		
delivered	SFR	depleted		
deliveries	SFR	deposit		
delivering	SFR	deposited		
delivery	SFR	deposits		
delta		depreciable	CF	
deluxe		depreciation	CF	
demand		depression		
demands		depth		

derived		destroy	
describe		destroyed	
described		destruction	
describes		detail	
describing		detailed	
description		details	
descriptive		determination	
design		determine	
designate		determined	
designated		determining	
designating		develop SF	
designation		developed SFR	
designed		developing SFR	
designs		development SFR	
desirable		developments SFR	
desire		develops SFR	
desired		device	
desires		devices	
desiring		devote	
desirous		devoted	
desk		dials	
desks		diameter	
despite		diamond	
destination		dictating	

dictation		directory	SFR	
did		disability		
didn't		disabled	SFR	
die		disappearance		
died		disappointed		
dies		disappointment		
differ		disaster		
difference		discharge		
differences		discharged		
different		discontinue		
difficult	SF	discontinued		
difficulties	SFR	discount	SFR	
difficulty	SFR	discounts	SFR	
digest		discover		
dimensions		discovered		
dining		discuss	SF	
dinner		discussed	SFR	
diploma		discussing	SFR	
direct	SF	discussion	SFR	
directed	SFR	discussions	SFR	
direction	SFR	disease		
directly	SFR	display		
director	SFR	displayed		
directors	SFR	displaying		

displays		dividend	CF
disposal		dividends	CF
dispose		divinity	
disposed		division	
disposition		divisions	
disregard	SFR	do	
distance		doctor	CF
distant		doctors	CF
distinctive	SFR	documents	
distinguished	SFR	does	
distribute	SF	doesn't	
distributed	SFR	doing	
distributing	SFR	dollar	
distribution	SFR	dollars	
distributor	SFR	domestic	
distributors	SFR	donation	
district		done	
districts		don't	
disturbed		door	
ditch		doors	
ditches		double	
ditto		doubled	
diversion		doubt	
divided		doubted	

down SF		drop	
downtown SFR		dropped	
dozen		dropping	
draft		drug	
drafts		druggist	
drain		drugs	
drainage		drum	
dramatic		drums	
draw		dry	
drawer		due	
drawing		dues	
drawings		duly	
drawn		dungarees	
dread		duplicate a., n.; v.	
drill		duplicated	
drilling		duplicating	
drills		duplication	
drink		duplicators	
drive		durable	
driven		during	
driver		duties	
drivers		duty	
driving		dwelling	

E

each	
eager	
earlier	
earliest	
early	
earn	
earned	
earnings	
earth	
ease	
easier	
easily	
east	
eastern	
easy	
economic SF	
economical SFR	
economically SFR	
economics SFR	
economy SF	
edge	

edition	
editor	
editorial	
editors	
educated SFR	
education SFR	
educational SFR	
educators SFR	
effect SF	
effective SFR	
effectively SFR	
effectiveness SFR	
effects SFR	
efficiency	
efficient	
efficiently	
effort	
efforts	
egg	
eggs	
eight	
eighteen	
eighth	
either	

E

elect	SF		emblem	
elected	SFR		emergencies	
election	SFR		emergency	
elections	SFR		emphasis	
electric			emphasize	
electrical			employ	SF
electricity			employed	SFR
electrification			employee	SFR
electronic			employees	SFR
electronics			employer	SFR
elementary			employers	SFR
elements			employing	SFR
elevator			employment	SFR
eleven			enable	SFR
eligibility			enabled	SFR
eligible			enables	SFR
eliminate			enabling	SFR
eliminated			enacted	
eliminates			enamel	
eliminating			enclose	SF
elimination			enclosed	SFR
else			enclosing	SFR
elsewhere	SFR		enclosure	SFR
embankment			enclosures	SFR

encountered	SFR	engineers	
encourage		enjoy	
encouraged		enjoyable	
encouragement		enjoyed	
encouraging		enjoying	
end		enjoyment	
endeavor		enough	SF
ended		enroll	
ending		enrolled	
endorse		enrollment	
endorsed		ensuing	
endorsement		enter	
endorsements		entered	
endowment		entering	
ends		enterprise	
enemy		entertainment	
energy		enthusiasm	CF
enforce		enthusiastic	CF
enforcement		entire	
engage		entirely	
engaged		entitle	
engine		entitled	
engineer		entrance n., v.	
engineering		entries	

entry		estimate	
envelope	SF	estimated	
envelopes	SFR	estimates	
equal		estimating	
equally		evaluate	SFR
equals		evaluating	SFR
equipment	SFR	evaluation	SFR
equipped	SFR	even	
equitable		evening	
equity		evenings	
equivalent		event	SF
erect		events	SFR
error		eventually	SFR
errors		ever	SF
escrow		every	SFR
especially	SFR	everyday	SFR
essential		everyone	SFR
essentially		everything	SFR
establish	SF	everywhere	SFR
established	SFR	evidence	
establishes	SFR	evidenced	
establishing	SFR	evident	
establishment	SFR	evidently	
estate	SFR	exact	

exactly		exciting	
examination		excluded	
examinations		excluding	
examine		exclusive	
examined		exclusively	
examining		excuse	
example		execute	
examples		executed	
exceed		execution	
exceeded		executive	
exceeding		executives	
exceeds		exempt	
excellent		exemption	
except		exercise	
excepting		exhausted	
exception		exhibit	
exceptional		exhibits	
exceptionally		exist	
exceptions		existence	
excess		existing	
excessive		exists	
exchange SFR		expand	
exchanged SFR		expanded	
excise		expanding	

expansion		explains	
expect SF		explanation	
expected SFR		explanatory	
expecting SFR		explore	
expedite		export	
expenditures		exposure	
expense SF		express	
expenses SFR		expressed	
expensive SFR		expressing	
experience SF		expression	
experienced SFR		extend	
experiences SFR		extended	
experiencing SFR		extending	
experiment		extension	
experiments		extensive	
expert		extensively	
experts		extent	
expiration		exterior	
expire		extra	
expired		extras	
expires		extreme	
explain		extremely	
explained		eye	
explaining		eyes	

F

fabric		fairly	
fabrics		fairness	
face		faith	
faced		faithfully	
faces		fall	
facilitate		falls	
facilities		familiar	
facility		familiarize	
facing		families	
fact SF		family	
factor		famous	
factories		fan	
factors		far	
factory		fare	
facts SFR		fares	
factual SFR		farm	
faculty		farmer	
fail		farmers	
failed		farming	
failure		farms	
fair		farther	
		fashion	
		fast	
		faster	

F

father	feet
fathers	fellow
fault	fellows
favor	fellowship
favorable	felt
favorably	fence
favored	few
favorite	fewer
fear	fiber
feasibility	fidelity
feasible	field
feature	fields
featured	fifteen 15
features	fifth 5
featuring	fifty 50
federal	fight
fee	figure SF
feed	figured SFR
feeding	figures SFR
feeds	figuring SFR
feel	file
feeling	filed
feels	files
fees	filing

fill		fires	
filled		firing	
filling		firm	
film		firmly	
films		firms	
final		first	
finally		fiscal	
finance		fish	
financed		fishery	
finances		fishing	
financial		fit	
financially		five	
financing		fixed	
find		fixture	
finding		flanges	
findings		flat	
finds		fleet	
fine		flight	
finest		flood	
finish		floor	
finished		flooring	
finishing		floors	
fir		flow	
fire		fluid	

fly		foremost	
flying		foresight	
foam		forest	
folder		forever SFR	
folders		forget	
folding		forgotten	
folks		form SF	
follow		formal SFR	
followed		format SFR	
following		formation SFR	
follows		formed SFR	
food		former SFR	
foods		formerly SFR	
foot		forms SFR	
football		formula SFR	
footwear		formulated SFR	
for		fort	
force		forth	
forced		forthcoming	
forces		fortunate	
forecast		fortunately	
forecasts		forty	
foregoing SFR		forum	
foreign		forward	

forwarded		from SF	
forwarding		front	
found SF		frozen	
foundation SFR		fruit	
four		fudge	
fourteen		fuel	
fourth		fulfill	
frame		fulfilled	
franchise		full	
frank		fullest	
frankly		fully	
free		fun	
freedom		function	
freeze		functions	
freight		fund	
frequency		fundamental	
frequent		funding	
frequently		funds	
fresh		funeral	
friend		furnace	
friendly		furnish	
friends		furnished	
friendship		furnishing	
fringe		furniture	

further		gave		
furthermore	SFR	general		
fuser		generally		
future		generated		
		generous		

G

gain		genuine	
gained		genuinely	
gains		get	
galley		gets	
gallon		getting	
gallons		giant	
game		gift	
games		gifts	
garage		girl	
garden		girls	
gardens		give	
gas		given	
gasoline		gives	
gate		giving	
gather		glad	
gathering		gladly	
gauge		glass	
		go SF	

gentlemen   CF

goal		graduating	SFR
goals		graduation	SFR
goes	SFR	grain	
going	SFR	grand	
gold		grant	
golden		granted	
golf		granting	
gone		grants	
good	SF	graphic	
goods	SFR	grass	
got		grateful	
gotten		gratifying	
governing	SFR	gratitude	
government	SFR	gray	
governmental	SFR	grazing	
governments	SFR	grease	
governor	SFR	great	SF
governors	SFR	greater	SFR
grace		greatest	SFR
grade		greatly	SFR
grades		green	
graduate	SF	greetings	
graduated	SFR	grocery	
graduates	SFR	gross	

G

ground	SF	gun	
grounds	SFR	guy	
group		gymnasium	
groups		gypsum	
grout			
grove		**H**	
groves			
grow		habitat	
growing		habits	
grown		had	
growth		half	
guarantee		hall	
guaranteed		hand	
guaranty		handbook	
guard		handicapped	
guess		handle	
guest		handled	
guests		handles	
guidance		handling	
guide		hands	
guidelines		handsome	
guides		handy	
guilty		hang	
gulf		happen	

happened		heard	
happens		hearing	
happiness		hearings	
happy		heart	
hard		hearty	
hardship		heat	
hardware		heater	
harvest		heating	
has SF		heavier	
hasten		heavy	
have SF		hedge	
haven't SFR		heels	
having SFR		height	
hazard		heirs	
hazards		held	
he SF		help	
head		helped	
headed		helpful	
heading		helping	
headquarters CF		helps	
heads		hence	
health		her	
healthy		here	
hear		hereafter SFR	

H

hereby	SFR		his	SF
herein	SFR		historical	
here's	SFR		history	
hereto			hit	
heretofore			hitting	
hereunder			hold	
herewith	SFR		holder	
he's	SFR		holders	
hesitate			holding	
hidden			holdings	
high			holds	
higher			hole	
highest			holes	
highlights			holiday	
highly			holidays	
highway			home	
highways			homeless	
hill			homes	
hills			honest	
him			honor	
himself			honorable	
hire			honorary	
hired			honored	
hiring			hope	SF

Word		Shorthand	Word		Shorthand
hoped	SFR		huge		
hopeful	SFR		human		
hopefully	SFR		hundred		
hopes	SFR		hundreds		
hoping	SFR		hungry		
horse			hunting		
horses			hurry		
hose			hurt		
hospital	SF		husband		
hospitality	SFR		hydroelectric		
hospitalization	SFR				
hospitals	SFR				
host					
hot			I		
hotel			ice		
hotels			I'd	SFR	
hour	SF		idea		
hours	SFR		ideal		
house			idealism		
household			ideas		
houses			identification		
housing			identified		
how	SF		identify		
however	SFR		if	SF	

I

I'll SFR		impressed	
ill		impression	
illness		impressive	
illustrated CF		imprint	
illustrates CF		imprinted	
illustration CF		improve SF	
illustrations CF		improved SFR	
I'm SFR		improvement SFR	
imagination		improvements SFR	
imagine		improving SFR	
immediate SF		in SF	
immediately SF		inability	
impact		inadequate	
impartial		inadvertently CF	
imperative		inasmuch SFR	
implement		incentive	
import		inch	
importance SF		inches	
important SF		incident	
imported		incidentally	
imports		inclined	
impose		include	
imposed		included	
impossible		includes	

including		indicates		
inclusion		indicating		
inclusive		indication		
income		individual	SF	
inconvenience	SFR	individually	SFR	
inconvenienced	SFR	individuals	SFR	
incorporated	CF	industrial	SFR	
incorporation	CF	industries	SFR	
incorrect		industry	SF	
increase		inexpensive	SFR	
increased		inflation		
increases		inflationary		
increasing		influence		
increasingly		inform	SFR	
incurred		informal	SFR	
indebtedness		information	SF	
indeed		informative	SFR	
indemnity		informed	SFR	
independence		informing	SFR	
independent		ingredients		
index		inhabitants		
indexed		inheritance		
indicate		initial		
indicated		initiate		

initiated		installations	
initiative		installed	
injured		installing	
injuries		installment	
injury		installments	
ink		instance	
inks		instances	
inland		instead	
inquire		institute	
inquired		institution	
inquiries		institutions	
inquiring		instruct SF	
inquiry		instructed SFR	
insert		instruction SFR	
inserted		instructions SFR	
inside		instructor SFR	
insist		instructors SFR	
insofar SFR		instrument	
inspect SF		instruments	
inspection SFR		insurance SFR	
inspector SFR		insure SFR	
inspiration		insured SFR	
install		insureds SFR	
installation		insuring SFR	

integrity		interview	
intellectual		interviews	
intelligent		into	
intend		introduce	
intended		introduced	
intensive		introducing	
intent		introduction	
intention		introductory	
intentions		inventories	
interchange SFR		inventory	
interest SF		invest	
interested SFR		invested	
interesting . SFR		investigate	
interests SFR		investigation	
interfere		investigations	
interim		investment	
interior		investments	
intermediate		investors	
internal		invitation SF	
international		invite SF	
interpretation		invited SFR	
interruption		inviting SFR	
interstate SFR		invoice	
interval		invoiced	

invoices		ivory	
involve			
involved			
involves		**J**	
involving			
iron		job	
irons		jobber	
irrigation		jobbers	
is SF		jobs	
island		join	
isn't SFR		joined	
issuance SFR		joining	
issue SF		joins	
issued SFR		joint	
issues SFR		jointly	
issuing SFR		journal	
it SF		judge	
item		judges	
itemized		judgment	
items		judiciary	
it's SFR		junior	
its SFR		jurisdiction	
itself SFR		jury	
I've SFR		just SF	
		justice SFR	

justification	SFR		kits	
justified	SFR		knew	
justify	SFR		know	
juvenile			knowing	
			knowledge	
			known	

K

| | | knows | |

keen				

L

keep			label	
keeping			labels	
keeps			labor	
kept			laboratory	
key			lack	
keys			ladies	
killed			lading	
killing			lady	
kilowatts			lake	
kind			lakes	
kindest			lamp	
kindly			lamps	
kinds			land	
king			lands	
kit				
kitchen				

J
K
L

lane		leader	
language		leaders	
lapse		leadership	
large		leading	
largely		leads	
larger		leaf	
largest		leaflet	
last		league	
lasting		learn	
late		learned	
later		learning	
latest		lease	
latter		leased	
laundry		leases	
law		leasing	
lawn		least	
laws		leather	
lawyer		leave	
lawyers		leaves	
lay		leaving	
layoff		lecture	
layoffs		lectures	
layout SFR		led	
lead		ledger	

left		liability	
leg		liable	
legal		liaison	
legislation	CF	liberal	
legislative	CF	liberty	
legislature	CF	libraries	
lend		library	
lender		license	
length		licensed	
lengths		licensees	
less		licenses	
lesser		licensing	
lesson		lien	
let		lies	
let's		lieu	
lets		lieutenant	
letter	SF	life	
letterhead	SFR	lifetime	SFR
lettering	SFR	light	
letters	SFR	lighting	
letting		lights	
level		like	
levels		likely	
liabilities		likewise	

limit		living	
limitation		load	
limitations		loaded	
limited		loading	
limits		loads	
line		loan	
lined		loans	
lines		local	
lining		localities	
liquid		locality	
liquidate		locally	
list		locate	
listed		located	
listen		locating	
listing		location	
listings		locations	
lists		lock	
literally		locks	
literature		lodge	
little		lodges	
live v., a.		log	
lived v., a.		logical	
lives v., n.		long	
livestock		longer	

look		lumber	
looked		lump	
looking		lunch	
looks		luncheon	
loop			
loose			
lose			

M

losing		machine	
loss		machinery	
losses		machines	
lost		made	
lot		magazine	
lots		magazines	
love		magnificent CF	
loved		mahogany	
lovely		mail	
low		mailed	
lower		mailing	
lowered		mailings	
lowest		main	
loyal		maintain	
loyalty		maintained	
lubrication		maintaining	
luck		maintains	

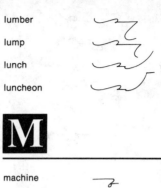

M

maintenance		manufacturer	SFR
major		manufacturers	SFR
majority		manufactures	SFR
make		manufacturing	SFR
maker		manuscript	
makers		many	
makes		map	
making		maple	
man		maps	
manage		margin	
managed		marine	
management		mark	
managements		marked	
manager		market	
managers		marketing	
managing		markets	
mandatory		marking	
manila		marks	
manner		married	
manpower		mass	
manual		master	
manuals		masters	
manufacture	SF	mat	
manufactured	SFR	match	

matching		measure	
material SF		measured	
materially SFR		measures	
materials SFR		meat	
mathematics CF		mechanical	
mats		mechanics	
matter		mechanism	
matters		media	
mattresses		medical	
maturity		medicare	
maximum		medicenter	
may		medicine	
maybe SFR		medium	
mayor		meet	
me		meeting	
meal		meetings	
meals		meets	
mean		member	
meaning		members	
meaningful		membership	
means		memberships	
meant		memo	
meantime SFR		memorandum	
meanwhile SFR		memorial	

memory		meters	
memos		method	
men		methods	
men's		metropolitan	
mental		microphone	
mention		middle	
mentioned		middling	
merchandise SF		midsemester	
merchandising SFR		might	
merchant		mighty	
merchants		mild	
mercury		mile	
mere		mileage	
merely		miles	
merger		military	
merit		milk	
merits		mill	
merry		million	
mesh		millions	
message		mills	
met		mimeographed	
metal		mind	
metals		minds	
meter		mine	

mineral		modest	
minerals		modification	
minimum		modified	
mining		moisture	
ministers		moment	
minor		money	
minute n., a.		moneys	
minutes		month	
mirror		monthly	
miscellaneous		months	
misplaced		moral	
miss		more SF	
missed		moreover SFR	
missing		morning	
mission		mornings	
mistake		mortgage SF	
misunderstanding SFR		mortgagee SFR	
mix		mortgagees SFR	
mixed		mortgages SFR	
mobilization		mortgagor SFR	
model		most	
models		mostly	
modern		motel	
modernization		motels	

mother		mutual	
mothers		mutually	
motion		my	
motor		myself	
motors			
mountain		**N**	
mounted			
mounting		name	
mouth		named	
move		namely	
moved		names	
movement		nation	
movements		national	
movers		nationally	
moves		nations	
movie		nationwide	
moving		native	
mowers		natural	
much		naturally	
mud		nature	
multiple		naval	
municipal		navy	
music		near	
must SF		nearby SFR	

nearest		newly	
nearly		news	
necessarily SFR		newsletter SFR	
necessary SF		newspaper SF	
necessitate		newspapers SFR	
necessity		next SF	
need		nice	
needed		nicely	
needless		night	
needs		nights	
neglect		nine	
neglected		ninety	
negotiated CF		ninth	
negotiations CF		no	
neighborhood		nominal	
neighboring		nominating	
neighbors		nomination	
neither		none	
net		nonpayment	
neutral		nonprofit	
never		noon	
nevertheless SFR		nor	
new		normal	
newest		normally	

N

north	~w	nurses	~e,
northern	~w	nursing	~e,
northwest	~w	nylon	~a,
not SF	—		
notation	~e		
note	~v		

noted	~v	oak	y y
notes	~v	object	y y
nothing SFR	~v	objection	y y
notice SF	~v	objective	y y
noticed SFR	~v	objectives	y y
notices SFR	~v	obligated	y y
notification	~v	obligation	y y
notified	~v	obligations	y y
notify	~v	observation SFR	y y
notifying	~v	observe SFR	y y
now	~v	observed SFR	y y
nuclear	~e	obtain	y
number SF	~v	obtainable	y y
numbered SFR	~v	obtained	y
numbering SFR	~v	obtaining	y
numbers SFR	~v	obvious	y
numerous	~v	obviously	y
nurse	~e,	occasion	v,

occasional		official	
occasionally		officially	
occasions		officials	
occupancy		offset	
occupation		often	
occupational		oil	
occupied		oils	
occupy		okay	
occur		old	
occurred		older	
occurs		omitted	
ocean		on	
odd		once SFR	
of SF		one SF	
off		ones SFR	
offer		only	
offered		open	
offering		opened	
offerings		opening	
offers		openings	
office		opens	
officer		operate	
officers		operated	
offices		operates	

O

operating		ordinary	
operation		organization SF	
operational		organizational SFR	
operations		organizations SFR	
operator		organized SFR	
operators		orientation	
opinion		origin	
opinions		original	
opportunities SFR		originally	
opportunity SF		originating	
opposed		orthopedic	
optimistic		other	
option		others	
optional		otherwise	
or		ought	
orange		ounce	
orchestra		our SF	
order SF		ours SFR	
ordered SFR		ourselves SFR	
ordering SFR		out SF	
orderly SFR		outcome SFR	
orders SFR		outdoor SFR	
ordinance		outfit SFR	
ordinarily		outlet SFR	

outlets	SFR	
outline	SFR	
outlined	SFR	
outlines	SFR	
outlining	SFR	
outlook	SFR	
output	SFR	
outside	SFR	
outstanding	SFR	
over		
overall		
overcome		
overdue		
overhead		
overlooked		
overpayment		
overseas		
oversight		
overwhelming		
owe		
owed		
own		
owned		
owner		

owners	
ownership	
owns	

P

pace	
pacific	
pack	
package	
packaged	
packages	
packaging	
packed	
packers	
packets	
packing	
pads	
page	
pages	
paid	
paint	
painted	
painting	

pair		participation SFR	
pairs		particular SF	
pallet		particularly SFR	
palletized		particulars SFR	
pamphlet		parties SFR	
pamphlets		partner SFR	
pan		partnership SFR	
panel		parts SFR	
paper		party SFR	
papers		pass	
par		passage	
paragraph		passed	
parcel		passenger	
parcels		passengers	
parent		passing	
parents		past	
parity		paste	
park		pasture	
parking		patent	
part SF		patience	
partial		patient	
participants SFR		patients	
participate SFR		patronage	
participating SFR		pattern	

patterns		percentages	
pay		perfect a., v.	
payable		perfectly	
payee		perform SFR	
paying		performance SFR	
payment		performed SFR	
payments		performing SFR	
payroll		perhaps	
pays		period	
peace		periodic	
peacetime SFR		periods	
peak		permanent	
pen		permissible	
penalty		permission	
pencils		permit	
pending		permits	
penny		permitted	
pens		permitting	
pension		person	
people		personal	
peoples		personality	
per		personalized	
percent		personally	
percentage		personnel	

persons	picking
pertaining	pickup
pertains	picture
pertinent	pictures
petition	piece
petitions	pieces
petroleum	pin
phase	pine
phases	pink
philosophy	pioneer
phone	pipe
phosphate	place
photo	placed
photograph	placement
photographs	placements
photos	places
photostat	placing
physical	plain
physician	plains
physicians	plaintiff
piano	plan
pianos	plane
pick	planned
picked	planning

plans		pointing	
plant		points	
planted		police	
planting		policies	
plants		policy	
plastic		policyholder	
plastics		policyholders	
plat		polio	
plate		political	
plates		pollution	
play		pool	
played		poor	
playing		popular	
pleasant		population	
please SF		populations	
pleased SFR		port	
pleasure		portable	
pledge		portfolio	
plenty		portion	
plumbing		portions	
plus		ports	
pocket		position	
point		positions	
pointed		positive	

possession		practically	
possibilities		practice	
possibility		practices	
possible		praise	
possibly		precedence	
post		preceding	
postage		precinct	
postal		precisely	
postcard		precision	
postcards		predict	
posted		prefer	
posting		preferably	
postmaster		preference	
postpaid		preferred	
posts		preliminary	
potential		premises	
potentials		premium	
poultry		premiums	
pound		prepaid	
pounds		preparation	
power		prepare	
powered		prepared	
powers		preparing	
practical		prepayment	

prescribed		pricer	
presence		prices	
present SF		pricing	
presentation SFR		pride	
presentations SFR		primarily	
presented SFR		primary	
presenting SFR		prime	
presently SFR		principal	
presents SFR		principle	
president		principles	
presidents		print	
press		printed	
presses		printer	
pressure		printing	
pressures		prints	
presume		prior	
pretty		priority	
prevent		privacy	
prevention		private	
preview		privilege	
previous		privileges	
previously		prize	
price		probability SFR	
priced		probable SF	

probably SFR		profession	
problem SF		professional	
problems SFR		professor	
procedure		profit	
procedures		profitable	
proceed		profits	
proceeding		program	
proceedings		programmed	
proceeds		programming	
process		programs	
processed		progress	
processes		progressive	
processing		project	
procurement		projected	
produce		projector	
produced		projects	
producers		prominent	
produces		promise	
producing		promised	
product SF		promises	
production SFR		promote	
productive SFR		promoted	
productivity SFR		promoting	
products SFR		promotion	

promotional		protective	
promotions		protects	
prompt SF		prototype	
promptly SFR		proud	
proof		prove	
proofs		proved	
proper		proven	
properly		proves	
properties		provide SF	
property		provided SFR	
proportion		provides SFR	
proposal		providing SFR	
proposals		proving	
propose		provision	
proposed		provisions	
proposition		proxy	
prorate		psychiatric CF	
prospect CF		psychology	
prospective CF		public SF	
prospects CF		publication SFR	
protect		publications SFR	
protected		publicity	
protecting		publish SF	
protection		published SFR	

publisher	SFR	
publishers	SFR	
publishing	SFR	
pump		
pumps		
punch		
punching		
pupils		
purchase		
purchased		
purchaser		
purchasers		
purchases		
purchasing		
pure		
purpose		
purposes		
pursuant		
pursue		
pursuing		
push		
put		
puts		
putting		

qualifications		
qualified		
qualify		
qualities	SFR	
quality	SF	
quantities	SFR	
quantity	SF	
quart		
quarter		
quarterly		
quarters		
quarts		
question	SF	
questionnaire	SFR	
questions	SFR	
quick		
quickly		
quiet		
quit		
quite		
quota		

quotation		ranges	
quotations		ranging	
quote		rank	
quoted		rapid	
quoting		rapidly	

R

		rapids	
		rare	
		rate	
race		rated	
radio		rates	
radios		rather	
rail		rating	
railroad		ratio	
railroads		raw	
railway		re	
rain		reach	
raise		reached	
raised		reaches	
raises		reaching	
raising		reaction	
ran		reactor	
ranch		read	
range		reader	
rangers		readers	

Q
R

readily		recent	
reading		recently	
reads		reception	
ready		recheck	
real		recipient	
realize		recipients	
realized		recognition	CF
realizing		recognize	CF
really		recognized	CF
rear		recommend	
reason		recommendation	
reasonable		recommendations	
reasonably		recommended	
reasons		recommending	
rebate		record	SF
recall		recorded	SFR
receipt		recorder	SFR
receipts		recording	SFR
receive	SF	records	SFR
received	SFR	recovery	
receiver	SFR	recreation	
receivers	SFR	recreational	
receives	SFR	recruiting	
receiving	SFR	red	

redemption		regard	SF	
reduce		regarding	SFR	
reduced		regardless	SFR	
reduces		regards	SFR	
reducing		region		
reduction		regional		
reductions		regions		
redwood		register		
refer		registered		
reference		registrar		
references		registration		
referendum		regret		
referred		regular	SF	
referring		regularly	SFR	
refers		regulation		
refining		regulations		
reflect		rehabilitation		
reflected		reimbursement		
reflects		reinstated	SFR	
refrigerated		reinsurance	SFR	
refund		rejected		
refunded		relate		
refuse		related		
refused		relates		

relating		remember	
relation		remembered	
relations		remind	
relationship		reminded	
relationships		reminder	
relative		remit	
relatively		remittance	
relay		remitted	
release		removal	
released		remove	
releases		removed	
reliable		removing	
relief		render	
relieved		rendered	
religious		rendering	
reluctant		renew	
rely		renewal	
remain		renewed	
remainder		rent	
remained		rental	
remaining		rentals	
remains		reorder SFR	
remarkable		repair	
remarks		repaired	

repairing		reprint	
repairs		reprints	
repay		reproduced	
repayment		reproduction	SFR
repeat		reputation	
replace		request	SF
replaced		requested	SFR
replacement		requesting	SFR
replacements		requests	SFR
replacing		require	SF
replies		required	SFR
reply		requirement	SFR
replying		requirements	SFR
report	SF	requires	SFR
reported	SFR	requiring	SFR
reporting	SFR	requisition	
reports	SFR	resale	
represent	SFR	research	
representation	SFR	reservation	SFR
representative	SFR	reservations	SFR
representatives	SFR	reserve	SFR
represented	SFR	reserved	SFR
representing	SFR	reserves	SFR
represents	SFR	reservoir	SFR

residence		restrictions	
residency		result SF	
resident		resulted SFR	
residential		resulting SFR	
residents		results SFR	
resolution		resume	
resolutions		retail	
resolve		retailer	
resolved		retailers	
resource		retain	
resources		retained	
respect SF		retaining	
respectfully SFR		retention	
respective SFR		retire	
respectively SFR		retirement	
respects SFR		return SF	
respond		returned SFR	
response SF		returning SFR	
responsibilities SFR		returns SFR	
responsibility SFR		revenue	
responsible SFR		revenues	
rest		reverse	
restraint		review	
restricted		reviewed	

reviewing		role	
revised		roll	
revision		rolls	
revisions		roof	
revolutionary		roofing	
rewarding		room	
ribbon		rooms	
ribbons		rose	
rich		roster	
rider		rotary	
riding		rough	
right		round	
rights		route	
ring		routes	
rings		routine	
rise		routing	
rising		royalty	
risk		rubber	
risks		rug	
river		rugs	
road		rule	
roads		rules	
rock		ruling	
rods		run	

running		sample	
runs		samples	
rural		sand	
rush		sanitary	
rust		sat	
		satisfaction SFR	
S		satisfactorily SFR	
		satisfactory SF	
		satisfied SFR	
sacrifice		satisfy SF	
safe		save	
safely		saves	
safety		saving	
sald		savings	
sailing		saw	
sailings		saws	
salaries		say	
salary		saying	
sale		says	
sales		scale	
salesman		scales	
salesmen		scattered	
salt		scene	
salvage		scenic	
same			

schedule	CF		seat	
scheduled	CF		seats	
schedules	CF		second	
scheduling	CF		secondary	
scholarship			secondly	
school			seconds	
schools			secret	
science			secretarial	SFR
sciences			secretaries	SFR
scientific			secretary	SF
scope			section	
score			sections	
scores			secure	
scotch			secured	
scrap			securing	
screen			securities	
screening			security	
screens			see	
seal			seeds	
seals			seeing	
search			seek	
season			seeking	
seasonal			seem	
seasons			seemed	

S

seems		sensational	
seen		sense	
seldom		sent	
select		separate a., v.	
selected		separately	
selecting		serial	
selection		series	
selective		serious	
self		seriously	
sell		serve SF	
sellers		served SFR	
selling		serves SFR	
sells		service SFR	
semester		serviced SFR	
semiannual		services SFR	
semiannually		servicing SFR	
seminar		serving SFR	
seminars		session	
senate		sessions	
senator		set	
senators		sets	
send SF		setting	
sending SFR		settle	
senior		settled	

settlement		sheet	
settlements		sheets	
setup		shelf	
seven	7	shift	
seventh		ship SF	
seventy	70	shipment SFR	
several		shipments SFR	
severe		shipped SFR	
severely		shipper SFR	
sewer		shippers SFR	
sewing		shipping SFR	
shade		ships SFR	
shaft		shirt	
shall SF		shirts	
shape		shoe	
share		shoes	
shareholder		shoot	
shareholders		shooting	
shares		shop	
sharing		shopping	
sharp		shops	
sharply		short SF	
she		shortage SFR	
sheep		shortages SFR	

shorter	SFR		significantly	CF
shorthand	SFR		signing	
shortly	SFR		signs	
shorts	SFR		silicon	
shot			silver	
should			similar	
show			simple	
showed			simplified	
showing			simplify	
shown			simply	
shows			simultaneously	
shut			since	
sick			sincere	
sickness			sincerely	CF
side			single	
sides			sit	
siding			site	
sight			sites	
sign			situation	SF
signature			situations	SFR
signatures			six	
signed			sixteen	
significance	CF		sixth	
significant	CF		sixty	

size	$\wp$	so		C
sized	$\wp$	soap		ξ
sizes	$\wp$	social		$\dot{\xi}$
sketch	$\int$	society		ξ_ρ
skiing	ξ	sod		ξ
skill	ξ	soft		ξ
skilled	$\xi_{,}$	soil		ϱ
skills	ξ_{ι}	soils		ϱ_ζ
skin	ξ	sold		ω
slack	φ	sole		ω
slacks	φ	solely		ω
slide	φ	solicit		ζ_ω
slight	φ	solid		ω
slightly	φ	solution		ζ_3
slip	ζ	solutions		ζ_3
slips	ζ_3	solve		ω_3
slow	ζ_ω	solved		$\omega^{\prime}$
small	$\sim$	solving		$\omega^{\prime}$
smaller	$\sim$	some		$\hbar$
smallest	$\sim_\nu$	someone	SFR	$\hbar\sqrt{}$
smart	ω	something	SFR	$\hbar^{\prime}$
smile	ω	sometime	SFR	$\hbar$
smooth	$\sim_\gamma$	sometimes	SFR	$\hbar\,C$
smoothly	$\sim_\rho$	somewhat	SFR	$\hbar\sqrt{}$

somewhere	SFR		speaking	
son			special	SF
sons			specialists	SFR
soon			specialized	SFR
sooner			specially	SFR
sorry			specific	SF
sort			specifically	SFR
sought			specification	SFR
sound			specifications	SFR
source			specified	SFR
sources			specify	SF
south			specimen	
southeast			speech	
southeastern			speeches	
southern			speed	
southwest			spend	
southwestern			spending	
space			spent	
spaced			spirit	
spacing			spiritual	
spare			spite	
speak			splendid	
speaker			split	
speakers			spoke	

sponsor		stamp	
sponsored		stamped	
sponsoring		stamps	
sponsors		stand SF	
spools		standard SFR	
sport		standardization SFR	
sporting		standards SFR	
sports		standing SFR	
spot		standpoint SFR	
spouse		stands SFR	
spray		staples	
spread		star	
spring		stars	
springs		start	
sprocket		started	
sprockets		starting	
square		starts	
stability		state SF	
stabilization		stated SFR	
staff		statement SFR	
stage		statements SFR	
stages		states SFR	
stainless		statewide SFR	
stake		stating SFR	

station		stimulate	
stationery		stimulating	
stations		stock	
statistical		stockholders	
statistics		stocking	
status SFR		stockpile	
statute		stocks	
statutes		stone	
statutory		stones	
stay		stop	
staying		stops	
steadily		storage	
steady		store	
steam		stored	
steel		stores	
stencil		stories	
stencils		storm	
stenographer		story	
stenographers		straight	
step		straighten	
steps		strategy	
stewardship		stream	
stickers		street	
still		streets	

strength		subdivision	
strengthen		subject	
stress		subjects	
stricken		submission	
strict		submit	
strictly		submitted	
strike		submitting	
strips		subscribe	
strive		subscriber	
strong		subscribers	
stronger		subscribing	
strongly		subscription	
structural		subscriptions	
structure		subsequent	
structures		subsidiary	
student		subsistence	
students		substantial	
studies		substantially	
study		substitute	
studying		substitution	
style		suburbs	
styled		succeed	
styles		succeeding	
subcommittee SFR		success SF	

successful	SFR		superintendents	
successfully	SFR		superior	
such			supervision	
sudden			supervisor	
sufficient			supervisors	
sufficiently			supervisory	
sugar			supplement	
suggest	SF		supplemental	
suggested	SFR		supplementary	
suggesting	SFR		supplemented	
suggestion	SFR		supplements	
suggestions	SFR		supplied	
suggests	SFR		supplier	
suit			suppliers	
suitable			supplies	
suited			supply	
suits			supplying	
sum			support	
summary			supported	
summer			supporting	
summons			suppose	
sun			supposed	
super			supreme	
superintendent			surcharge	

sure	SF		symptoms	
surely	SFR		system	
surface			systems	
surfaces				

T

surgeon				
surgeons		tab		
surgery		table		
surgical		tables		
surplus		tag		
surpluses		tags		
surprise		tailored		
surrender		take		
surrounding		taken		
survey		takes		
surveys		taking		
suspect n., v.		talent		
suspended		talents		
sustained		talk		
swimming		talked		
swing		talking		
switch		talks		
switches		tank		
sympathetic		tanks		
sympathy				

T

tape	*ℓ*	teeth	
tariff		telegram	
tariffs		telephone	
task		telephones	
tasks		television	
taught		tell	
tax		telling	
taxable		tells	
taxation		temperature	
taxed		temporarily	
taxes		temporary	
taxpayer		ten	*10*
taxpayers		tend	
teach		tennis	
teacher		tentative	
teachers		tentatively	
teaching		tenth	*10*
team		term	
tear		terminal	
n., v.			
technical		terminate	
technicians		terminated	
technique		termination	
techniques		terms	
technology		territory	

test		theory	
tested		there SF	
testified		thereafter SFR	
testimony		thereby SFR	
testing		therefore SFR	
tests		therein SFR	
text		thereof SFR	
textbook		thereon SFR	
textbooks		there's SFR	
textile		thereto SFR	
than SF		thermal	
thank SF		these	
thanking SFR		they	
thanks SFR		they'll SFR	
that SF		they're SFR	
that's SFR		thickness	
the SF		thin	
theater		thing SF	
theft		things SFR	
their SF		think SF	
them SF		thinking SFR	
theme		third	3
themselves SFR		thirteen	13
then SF		thirty	30

this		times SFR	
thorough		timing SFR	
thoroughly		tips	
those		tire	
though		tires	
thought		title	
thoughtful		titles	
thoughtfulness		to	
thoughts		today	
thousand		today's	
thousands		toe	
three		together	
through		told	
throughout SF		tomorrow	
throw		ton	
thrown		tons	
thus		too	
ticket		took	
tickets		tool	
tie		tools	
tile		tooth	
timber		top	
time SF		topic	
timely SFR		topics	

tops		trading	
tornado		traffic	
total		trailer	
totaled		trailers	
totaling		train	
totally		trained	
totals		training	
touch		transaction	
tough		transactions	
tour		transcript	
tours		transcription	
toward		transfer	
towards		transferred	
tower		transferring	
town		transfers	
towns		transformer SFR	
township		transistors	
toy		transit	
toys		transition	
track		transmission	
tracks		transmittal	
tract		transport	
tractor		transportation	
trade		travel	

traveling		trucking	
tray		trucks	
trays		true	
treasurer		truly	
treasury		trust	
treat		trustee	
treated		trustees	
treatment		trusting	
treaty		truth	
tree		try	
trees		trying	
tremendous		tube	
tremendously		tuberculosis	
trend		tubes	
trends		tuition	
trial		turn	
tried		turned	
trim		turning	
trip		turnover	
triplicate n., v.		turns	
trips		twelve	12
trouble		twenty	20
troubles		twice	
truck		twin	

two		understood	
type		undertake	
typed		undertaken	
types		undertaking	
typewriter		underway	
typewriters		underwrite	
typewriting		underwriters	
typical		underwriting	
typing		undoubtedly	
typist		undue	
typists		unearned	
		unemployed SFR	
		unemployment SFR	

U

		unfair	
ultimate		unfortunate	
ultimately		unfortunately	
unable SFR		uniform SFR	
unanimously		union	
unchanged SFR		unions	
under		unique	
undergraduate SFR		unit	
understand SFR		united	
understandable SFR		unitized	
understanding SFR		units	

U

universal		useful	
universities		user	
university		users	
unless		uses	
unloading		using	
unnecessary SFR		usual	
unpaid		usually	
until		utilities	
unused		utility	
unusual		utilization	
unusually		utilize	
up		utilized	
upland		utilizing	
upon		utmost	
upper			
urban			
urge		**V**	
urged			
urgent		vacancies	
urgently		vacancy	
urging		vacant	
us		vacation	
use		vacations	
used		vacuum	
		valid	

validity		versus	
valley		vertical	
valuable SFR		very SF	
valuation SFR		vessel	
value SF		vessels	
valued SFR		veteran	
values SFR		veterans	
valve		via	
valves		vice	
van		vicinity	
vapor		victory	
varied		view	
variety		viewer	
various		views	
vary		vigor	
vast		violation	
vehicle		violations	
vehicles		virtually	
vendor		visible	
vendors		visit	
venture		visited	
verify		visiting	
versatile		visitors	
versatility		visits	

V

visual		walk	
vital		wall	
vitally		walls	
vocational		walnut	
voice		want SF	
voltage		wanted SFR	
volume		wants SFR	
volumes		war	
voluntary		ward	
volunteer		wardrobe	
vote		warehouse	
voted		warehousemen	
voters		warm	
votes		warning	
voting		warrant	
voucher		warranty	

W

wage		was SF	
wages		wash	
wait		washing	
waiting		waste	
waiver		watch	
		watching	
		water	
		waters	

watershed		west	
wax		western	
way		wet	
ways		we've SFR	
we		what SF	
wealth		whatever SFR	
wear		what's SFR	
weather		whatsoever SFR	
we'd SFR		wheat	
week		wheel	
weekend		wheels	
weekly		when SF	
weeks		whenever SFR	
weighing		where SF	
weight		whereas SFR	
weights		whereby SFR	
welcome		wherein SFR	
welcoming		wherever SFR	
welfare		whether	
we'll SFR		which SF	
well SF		whichever SFR	
went		while SF	
we're SFR		white	
were		who	

W

whole		wish	
wholesale		wishes	
wholly		wishing	
whom		wit	
whose		with SF	
why SF		withdraw SFR	
wide		withdrawal SFR	
widely		withdrawals SFR	
wider		withdrawn SFR	
width		withheld SFR	
wife		withholding SFR	
wildlife		within SFR	
will SF		without SFR	
willing SFR		wives	
willingness SFR		woman	
win		women	
wind n., v.		women's	
window		won SF	
windows		wonder	
winners		wonderful	
winter		wondering	
wire		won't	
wiring		wood	
wise		wool	

word		write	
wording		writer	
words		writers	
work SF		writes	
workbook SFR		writing	
worked SFR		written	
worker SFR		wrong	
workers SFR		wrote	
working SFR			

X

workmanship SFR			
workmen's SFR			
works SFR		x-ray	
workshop SFR			

Y

world			
worlds			
worn		yard	
worry		yards	
worth SF		year	
worthwhile SFR		yearly	
worthy SFR		years	
would SF		yellow	
wouldn't SFR		yes	
wrap		yesterday	
wrapping		yet	

X-Y

yield	
yields	
you	
you'd SFR	
you'll SFR	
young	
youngsters	
your SF	
you're SFR	
yours SFR	
yourself SFR	
youth	
you've SFR	

Z

zone	
zoning	

100 COMMON PHRASES

about the		I will	
and the		I will be able	
appreciate your		I would	
are not		if you	
as you		in order	
at the		in our	
at this		in the	
by the		in this	
can be		in your	
do not		in your letter	
for the		is not	
for this		is the	
for you		it is	
for your		it is not	
from the		it was	
from you		it will	
has been		it will be	
have been		it would	
hope that		may be	
I am		of our	
I have		of the	
I have been		of these	
I hope		of this	

111

Z

of your		to us	
on the		to you	
on this		to your	
on your		we are	
one of		we are not	
one of our		we can	
should be		we do	
thank you		we have	
thank you for		we have been	
thank you for the		we will	
thank you for your letter		we will be able	
that the		we would	
that we		we would appreciate your	
that you		we would be	
there are		we would like	
there is		will be	
this is		with the	
this is not		with you	
this is the		with your	
to be		would be	
to have		would like	
to our		you are	
to the		you can	
to this		you have	

you have been		you will be	
you may		you would	
you will		your letter	

SPEEDFORMS & PUNCTUATION

a, an	.	associate	
able		at, it	
about		attention	
accept		be, been, by	
accord		business	
active, activity		can	
administer		certificate, certify	
advance		chairman	
advantage		change	
advertise		committee	
advice, advise		company	
affect, after		condition	
agriculture		consider	
am, more	—	construct	
amount		contact	
and		contain	
announce		contract	
anxious		contribute	
any		control	
appreciate		convenience, convenient	
approximate		convention	
are, hour, our		correspond, correspondence	
as, his, is		count	

custom		experience	
deliver		fact, if	
department		figure	
develop		form, from	
difficult		found	
direct		go, good	
discuss		govern	
distinct, distinguish		graduate	
distribute		great	
down		ground	
economic, economy		has	
educate		have, with	
effect		he	
elect		hope	
employ		hospital	
enclose		how, out	
enough		immediate, immediately	
envelope		importance, important	
equip		improve	
establish		in, not	
event		individual	
ever		industry	
expect		information	
expense		inspect, newspaper	

instruct		probable, problem	
interest		product	
invitation, invite		prompt	
issue		provide	
just		public, publish	
letter		quality	
manufacture		quantity	
material		question	
merchandise		receive	
mortgage		record	
must		regard	
necessary		regular	
next		report	
notice		request	
number		require	
of		respect	
one, won		response	
opportunity		result	
order		return	
organization, organize		satisfactory, satisfy	
part		secretary	
particular		send	
please		serve	
present		shall, ship	

116

short	✓	time	
situate, situation		value	
special		very	
specific, specify		want	
stand		was	
state		well, will	
success		what	
suggest		when	
sure		where	
than, then		which	
thank, think		while	
that		why	
the		work	
their, there		worth	
them		would	
thing		your	
throughout			

Punctuation

Capitalization	—	Parentheses	( )
Dash	M	Period	\
Hyphen	∧	Question Mark	∨
Paragraph	>		

117

DAYS OF THE WEEK / MONTHS OF THE YEAR

Days

Sunday	⟨shorthand⟩	Thursday	⟨shorthand⟩
Monday	⟨shorthand⟩	Friday	⟨shorthand⟩
Tuesday	⟨shorthand⟩	Saturday	⟨shorthand⟩
Wednesday	⟨shorthand⟩		

Months

January	⟨shorthand⟩	July	⟨shorthand⟩
February	⟨shorthand⟩	August	⟨shorthand⟩
March	⟨shorthand⟩	September	⟨shorthand⟩
April	⟨shorthand⟩	October	⟨shorthand⟩
May	⟨shorthand⟩	November	⟨shorthand⟩
June	⟨shorthand⟩	December	⟨shorthand⟩

EXAMPLES:

On the 8th of July

⟨shorthand⟩

On July 8

⟨shorthand⟩

200 COMMON SURNAMES

Adams		Campbell	
Alexander		Carlson	
Allen		Carpenter	
Anderson		Carr	
Andrews		Carroll	
Armstrong		Carter	
Arnold		Chapman	
Bailey		Clark	
Baker		Cohen	
Barnes		Cole	
Bell		Coleman	
Bennett		Collins	
Berry		Cook	
Bishop		Cooper	
Black		Cox	
Boyd		Crawford	
Bradley		Cunningham	
Brooks		Davis	
Brown		Day	
Bryant		Dean	
Burke		Dixon	
Burns		Duncan	
Butler		Dunn	

Edwards		Hanson	
Elliott		Harper	
Ellis		Harris	
Evans		Harrison	
Ferguson		Hart	
Fisher		Harvey	
Ford		Hawkins	
Foster		Hayes	
Fox		Henderson	
Freeman		Henry	
Fuller		Hicks	
Gardner		Hill	
Gibson		Hoffman	
Gilbert		Holmes	
Gordon		Howard	
Graham		Hudson	
Grant		Hughes	
Gray		Hunt	
Green		Hunter	
Greene		Jackson	
Griffin		James	
Hall		Jenkins	
Hamilton		Jensen	
Hansen		Johnson	

Johnston		Montgomery	
Jones		Moore	
Jordan		Morgan	
Kelley		Morris	
Kelly		Morrison	
Kennedy		Murphy	
King		Murray	
Knight		Myers	
Lane		Nelson	
Larson		Nichols	
Lawrence		O'Brien	
Lee		Olson	
Lewis		Owens	
Long		Palmer	
Lynch		Parker	
Marshall		Patterson	
Martin		Payne	
Mason		Perkins	
McCarthy		Perry	
McDonald		Peters	
Meyer		Peterson	
Miller		Phillips	
Mills		Pierce	
Mitchell		Porter	

Powell		Smith	
Price		Snyder	
Ray		Spencer	
Reed		Stephens	
Reynolds		Stevens	
Rice		Stewart	
Richards		Stone	
Richardson		Taylor	
Riley		Thomas	
Roberts		Thompson	
Robertson		Tucker	
Robinson		Turner	
Rogers		Wagner	
Rose		Walker	
Ross		Wallace	
Russell		Walsh	
Ryan		Warren	
Sanders		Washington	
Schmidt		Watkins	
Schneider		Watson	
Schultz		Weaver	
Shaw		Webb	
Simmons		Weber	
Simpson		Welch	

122

Wells		Willis	
West		Wilson	
Wheeler		Wood	
White		Wright	
Williams		Young	

FREQUENT ABBREVIATIONS

a.m.		Hundred Thousand	
America		Hundred Thousand Dollars	
American		Incorporated	
Avenue		Million	
Billion		Million Dollars	
Boulevard		O'clock	
Cent		OK (okay)	
Cents		Ordinal Numbers	
C.O.D.	cod	Percent	
Dollar		p.m.	
Dollars		P.O. Box	
Dollars and Cents		Railroad	
English		Street	
etc.		Thousand	
f.o.b.		Thousand Dollars	
Fractions		TV	
Hundred		U.S.	
Hundred Dollars		U.S.A.	

CORRESPONDENCE FORMS

Salutations

Dear		Dr.	
Dear Dr.		Gentlemen	
Dear Madam		Miss	
Dear Miss		Mr.	
Dear Mr.		Mrs.	
Dear Mrs.		Ms.	
Dear Sir			

Complimentary Closings

Cordially		Very sincerely yours	
Cordially yours		Very truly yours	
Most sincerely		Yours cordially	
Respectfully yours		Yours sincerely	
Sincerely		Yours truly	
Sincerely yours		Yours very truly	

(Abbreviation applies even though the above combinations are reversed, e.g., "Yours cordially.")

Other Correspondence Elements

Airmail	Parcel Post
Air Parcel Post	Please Forward
Attention	Printed Matter
cc	P.S.
Certified	Regard
Do Not Bend	Registered
Enclosure	Return Receipt Requested
First Class	Special Delivery
Fragile	Special Handling
Insured	Subject

126

RECOMMENDED STATE ABBREVIATIONS

Alabama	AL	Mississippi	MS
Alaska	AK	Missouri	MO
Arizona	AZ	Montana	MT
Arkansas	AR	Nebraska	NE
California	CA	Nevada	NV
Colorado	CO	New Hampshire	NH
Connecticut	CT	New Jersey	NJ
Delaware	DE	New Mexico	NM
Florida	FL	New York	NY
Georgia	GA	North Carolina	NC
Hawaii	HI	North Dakota	ND
Idaho	ID	Ohio	OH
Illinois	IL	Oklahoma	OK
Indiana	IN	Oregon	OR
Iowa	IA	Pennsylvania	PA
Kansas	KS	Rhode Island	RI
Kentucky	KY	South Carolina	SC
Louisiana	LA	South Dakota	SD
Maine	ME	Tennessee	TN
Maryland	MD	Texas	TX
Massachusetts	MA	Utah	UT
Michigan	MI	Vermont	VT
Minnesota	MN	Virginia	VA

127

| Washington | WA | | Wisconsin | WI | |
| West Virginia | WV | | Wyoming | WY | |

Additional Geographic Abbreviations

Alberta	AB		Northwest Territories	NT	
British Columbia	BC		Nova Scotia	NS	
Canal Zone	CZ		Ontario	ON	
District of Columbia	DC		Prince Edward Island	PE	
Guam	GU		Puerto Rico	PR	
Labrador	LB		Quebec	PQ	
Manitoba	MB		Saskatchewan	SK	
New Brunswick	NB		Virgin Islands	VI	
Newfoundland	NF		Yukon Territory	YT	

RANALLY METRO AREAS IN THE UNITED STATES

Akron	OH		Birmingham	AL	
Albany	NY		Boston	MA	
Albuquerque	NM		Bradenton	FL	
Allentown	PA		Bridgeport	CT	
Altoona	PA		Buffalo	NY	
Amarillo	TX		Canton	OH	
Anchorage	AK		Cedar Rapids	IA	
Anderson	IN		Champaign	IL	
Appleton	WI		Charleston	WV	
Asheville	NC		Charlotte	NC	
Ashland	KY		Chattanooga	TN	
Atlanta	GA		Chicago	IL	
Atlantic City	NJ		Cincinnati	OH	
Augusta	GA		Clearwater	FL	
Austin	TX		Cleveland	OH	
Bakersfield	CA		Colorado Springs	CO	
Baltimore	MD		Columbia	SC	
Baton Rouge	LA		Columbus	OH	
Battle Creek	MI		Corpus Christi	TX	
Beaumont	TX		Council Bluffs	IA	
Bethlehem	PA		Dallas	TX	
Biloxi	MS		Davenport	IA	
Binghamton	NY		Dayton	OH	

Daytona Beach	FL		Gulfport	MS
Decatur	IL		Hamilton	OH
Denver	CO		Hampton	VA
Des Moines	IA		Harrisburg	PA
Detroit	MI		Hartford	CT
Duluth	MN		High Point	NC
Durham	NC		Holyoke	MA
El Paso	TX		Honolulu	HI
Erie	PA		Hopewell	VA
Eugene	OR		Houston	TX
Evansville	IN		Huntington	WV
Fall River	MA		Huntsville	AL
Fayetteville	NC		Indianapolis	IN
Fitchburg	MA		Jackson	MS
Flint	MI		Jacksonville	FL
Ft. Lauderdale	FL		Johnstown	PA
Ft. Wayne	IN		Kalamazoo	MI
Ft. Worth	TX		Kansas City	MO
Fresno	CA		Knoxville	TN
Galveston	TX		Lake Charles	LA
Grand Rapids	MI		Lancaster	PA
Green Bay	WI		Lansing	MI
Greensboro	NC		Las Vegas	NV
Greenville	SC		Lawton	OK

Leominster	MA		Muskegon	MI
Lexington	KY		Nashville	TN
Lincoln	NE		New Bedford	MA
Little Rock	AR		New Britain	CT
Los Angeles	CA		Newburgh	NY
Louisville	KY		New Haven	CT
Lubbock	TX		New London	CT
Macon	GA		New Orleans	LA
Madison	WI		Newport News	VA
Manchester	NH		New York	NY
Mansfield	OH		Niagara Falls	NY
Massillon	OH		Norfolk	VA
Memphis	TN		Norwich	CT
Meriden	CT		Oakland	CA
Miami	FL		Oak Ridge	TN
Milwaukee	WI		Ogden	UT
Minneapolis	MN		Oklahoma City	OK
Mobile	AL		Omaha	NE
Modesto	CA		Orlando	FL
Moline	IL		Oxnard	CA
Monroe	LA		Pawtucket	RI
Monterey	CA		Pensacola	FL
Montgomery	AL		Peoria	IL
Muncie	IN		Petersburg	VA

Philadelphia	PA		St. Louis	MO	
Phoenix	AZ		St. Paul	MN	
Pittsburgh	PA		St. Petersburg	FL	
Pittsfield	MA		Salem	OR	
Port Arthur	TX		Salt Lake City	UT	
Portland	OR		San Antonio	TX	
Portsmouth	VA		San Bernardino	CA	
Poughkeepsie	NY		San Diego	CA	
Providence	RI		San Francisco	CA	
Provo	UT		San Jose	CA	
Pueblo	CO		Santa Barbara	CA	
Racine	WI		Sarasota	FL	
Raleigh	NC		Savannah	GA	
Reading	PA		Schenectady	NY	
Reno	NV		Scranton	PA	
Richmond	VA		Seattle	WA	
Riverside	CA		Shreveport	LA	
Roanoke	VA		South Bend	IN	
Rochester	NY		Spokane	WA	
Rockford	IL		Springfield	MA	
Rock Island	IL		Steubenville	OH	
Rome	NY		Stockton	CA	
Sacramento	CA		Superior	WI	
Saginaw	MI		Syracuse	NY	

132

Tacoma	WA		Washington	DC	
Tampa	FL		Waterbury	CT	
Terre Haute	IN		Waterloo	IA	
Texas City	TX		Weirton	WV	
Toledo	OH		West Palm Beach	FL	
Topeka	KS		Wheeling	WV	
Trenton	NJ		Wichita	KS	
Troy	NY		Wichita Falls	TX	
Tucson	AZ		Wilkes-Barre	PA	
Tulsa	OK		Wilmington	DE	
Tuscaloosa	AL		Winston-Salem	NC	
Urbana	IL		Woonsocket	RI	
Utica	NY		Worcester	MA	
Ventura	CA		York	PA	
Waco	TX		Youngstown	OH	
Warren	OH				

"Ranally Metro. Areas Ranked by Population, 1970," *1972 Commercial Atlas & Marketing Guide*, edited by Richard L. Forstall (Chicago: Rand McNally and Company, 1972), p. 46.

LARGEST METROPOLITAN AREAS AND CITIES OF THE WORLD

Athens,
Greece

Bangkok,
Thailand

Barcelona,
Spain

Berlin,
Germany

Birmingham,
England

Bombay,
India

Brussels,
Belgium

Budapest,
Hungary

Buenos Aires,
Argentina

Cairo,
Egypt

Calcutta,
India

Delhi,
India

Djakarta,
Indonesia

Essen,
Germany

Glasgow,
Scotland

Hamburg,
Germany

Havana,
Cuba

Istanbul,
Turkey

Johannesburg,
South Africa

Leningrad,
Russia

Lima,
Peru

Liverpool,
England

London,
England

Madras,
India

Madrid,
Spain

Manchester,
England

Manila,
Philippines

Melbourne,
Australia

Mexico City,
Mexico

Milan,
Italy

Montreal,
Canada

Moscow,
Russia

Osaka, Japan		Shanghai, China	
Paris, France		Sydney, Australia	
Peking, China		Taipeh, Taiwan	
Rio de Janeiro, Brazil		Tehran, Iran	
Rome, Italy		Tokyo, Japan	
Saigon, Vietnam		Toronto, Canada	
Santiago, Chile		Victoria, Hong Kong	
Sao Paulo, Brazil		Vienna, Austria	
Seoul, Korea		Warsaw, Poland	

"Largest Metropolitan Areas and Cities of the World, 1968," *1972 Commercial Atlas & Marketing Guide*, edited by Richard L. Forstall (Chicago: Rand McNally and Company, 1972), p. 593

1st 100		2d 100		3d 100	
the	so	send	every	home	come
of	there	good	area	paid	past
to	very	much	because	credit	write
and	other	under	day	following	concerning
in	should	what	must	both	within
you	no	hope	into	able	look
a	information	first	way	pay	position
for	year	state	form	where	case
we	office	get	same	members	week
your	more	just	last	copies	offer
that	me	find	days	full	recent
is	enclosed	help	next	general	system
be	some	its	three	him	back
this	service	possible	necessary	free	prices
will	am	interest	present	note	rate
on	business	insurance	shall	believe	set
have	now	date	feel	list	building
our	their	well	let	committee	items
are	also	over	here	payment	federal
I	know	sales	future	equipment	customers
with	about	number	forward	few	while
as	up	since	course	without	type
it	company	cost	report	application	basis
at	were	could	city	sent	employees
by	them	however	people	soon	important
or	who	available	sure	stock	book
not	out	return	those	until	long
if	make	school	part	own	personal
which	when	amount	complete	public	property
would	he	per	request	high	invoice
from	than	after	month	attached	provide
us	made	give	used	board	name
an	each	through	wish	enclosing	think
has	only	policy	matter	hospital	having
all	my	price	again	regarding	better
was	thank	best	additional	money	reply
can	two	see	call	pleased	receipt
any	copy	want	opportunity	given	great
been	department	during	today	card	loan
time	many	need	might	receive	increase
one	like	before	percent	life	several
these	had	meeting	special	attention	supply
letter	such	take	upon	total	less
may	his	further	interested	period	charge
please	work	received	then	tax	national
do	most	how	account	months	products
new	use	above	line	advise	contract
order	program	being	mail	job	happy
but	appreciate	plan	material	making	therefore
they	years	check	due	bill	association

4th 100		5th 100		6th 100	
questions	market	suggest	store	say	enough
change	place	meet	books	answer	half
too	statement	reason	end	act	needed
contact	thanks	working	sale	action	open
division	why	dealers	point	benefit	yet
done	fact	room	writing	shipped	increased
value	issue	training	advertising	six	facilities
keep	delivery	either	consideration	wishes	product
member	production	large	planning	doctor	changes
assistance	whether	subject	agency	envelope	connection
even	addition	costs	fine	found	operations
going	required	immediately	balance	her	provided
group	states	low	said	item	rather
requirements	annual	notice	ago	plant	paper
did	continue	care	always	purpose	particular
four	problems	convenience	law	times	entire
government	college	study	looking	proposed	expect
companies	current	weeks	old	receiving	far
county	five	regular	taken	telephone	means
management	visit	administration	never	tell	she
students	record	control	once	written	trade
held	small	little	trust	cases	model
right	claim	put	world	class	sample
services	ever	cover	box	off	unable
purchase	size	district	development	approval	areas
shipment	cooperation	hear	community	doing	bonds
still	organization	along	defense	include	cents
local	field	benefits	file	loss	helpful
requested	serve	desire	returned	perhaps	listed
records	representative	page	appreciated	understand	sold
does	section	pleasure	construction	attend	thought
bank	regards	cash	machine	labor	average
another	various	dated	second	bring	funds
water	membership	orders	address	personnel	sell
certainly	recently	family	merchandise	convention	you'll
education	don't	project	read	investment	result
glad	experience	already	oil	certain	below
go	men	covering	asked	employment	including
problem	savings	direct	unit	prior	indicated
reference	sending	premium	down	student	reserve
effective	customer	protection	effort	furnish	together
plans	probably	schedule	hand	sincerely	short
letters	manager	inquiry	quality	situation	director
needs	staff	original	ten	against	discuss
operation	rates	question	issued	commission	immediate
show	cannot	real	sheet	executive	monthly
between	kind	completed	become	others	policies
income	approximately	fill	dealer	reports	agreement
president	power	forms	individual	street	materials
ask	shown	industry	support	air	post

138

7th 100		8th 100		9th 100	
unless	lot	idea	accounting	fair	bills
effect	suggestions	million	gives	files	cards
least	teachers	regret	ideas	growth	developed
programs	big	coming	it's	industrial	foreign
promptly	delay	council	later	profit	housing
run	electric	details	mailed	returning	instructions
expense	ship	final	minimum	seems	known
man	using	gas	obligation	start	left
person	accept	getting	security	agree	manner
success	approved	morning	similar	conference	organizations
understanding	correct	payments	taxes	correspondence	personally
buy	extra	placed	enclose	handle	purposes
country	giving	among	farm	inch	season
handling	opinion	considered	remember	indicate	self
major	successful	continued	top	steel	teaching
quite	data	directly	war	supplies	carbon
showing	excellent	easy	arrangements	volume	children
things	interesting	head	machines	acknowledge	claims
yourself	space	limited	methods	apply	comments
health	try	regard	save	around	friends
included	discount	force	suggested	carry	offered
remain	follows	hours	activities	chairman	permit
according	herewith	involved	appreciation	factory	private
agent	mind	late	early	feet	procedure
consider	plus	near	expenses	spring	provisions
fee	united	require	hold	title	samples
house	financial	selling	offices	added	article
outstanding	firm	station	practice	based	commercial
persons	addressed	assist	south	court	food
prepared	called	except	submitted	distribution	level
regulations	corporation	express	view	fully	share
research	land	greatly	advantage	particularly	checks
results	lines	news	conditions	progress	convenient
sign	mailing	postage	friend	separate	deal
hesitate	method	ready	brochure	accordance	demand
something	operating	sorry	charges	asking	dozen
certificate	schools	accounts	clear	close	makes
prompt	terms	beginning	discussed	determine	manual
summer	advance	bureau	fire	facts	miss
advised	anything	designed	mentioned	furnished	seeing
assure	car	obtain	center	kindly	active
examination	catalog	proposal	different	retail	agents
freight	review	provides	especially	basic	extended
hearing	signed	truck	medical	concerned	filing
net	taking	booklet	parts	features	maintenance
north	throughout	condition	process	greater	shipping
proper	units	dollars	satisfactory	invitation	test
standard	estate	established	welcome	respect	third
although	event	picture	bulletin	series	trip
coverage	fall	specific	deposit	serving	campaign

10th 100   11th 100   12th 100

classes	press	damage	quickly	liability	worth
follow	previous	develop	refer	manufacturers	allow
higher	stores	difficult	shows	nature	associations
quantity	told	educational	subscription	qualified	automobile
range	town	evening	types	realize	certified
secretary	accident	I'm	club	requests	citizens
valuable	arrange	increases	courses	submit	confidence
yours	branch	informed	extend	thousands	described
capital	completely	offering	motor	turn	double
everything	daily	performance	nothing	calls	earnings
example	maximum	release	officer	desk	fees
age	portion	risk	story	drive	figures
central	purchased	substantial	sufficient	drop	green
cut	radio	teacher	survey	filed	highly
decision	responsibility	almost	wrote	floor	potential
faculty	source	checking	appears	generally	providing
longer	thing	design	authorized	groups	reasons
side	civil	indeed	blank	hour	secure
weekly	economic	phone	budget	join	that's
west	efforts	safety	directors	manufacture	thirty
away	employee	served	doubt	numbers	treasury
banks	engineering	stated	endorsement	papers	wanted
code	goods	whatever	exchange	paying	accepted
color	grade	words	fiscal	possibly	accordingly
congress	manufacturing	analysis	hard	pounds	cause
considerable	meetings	build	inform	reading	enjoy
conversation	points	church	international	representatives	excess
covered	revenue	entitled	participation	seem	explain
forwarded	sheets	instead	procedures	selected	felt
lease	television	license	promotion	step	figure
mortgage	travel	literature	published	storage	finance
officers	trouble	presented	recommend	western	handled
payable	actually	relative	replacement	amendment	heard
printed	ahead	reported	salary	buying	latest
professional	appropriate	requesting	single	contribution	move
thus	base	road	thanking	enable	pages
transportation	earliest	sincere	whom	face	prove
actual	kindest	term	applied	learn	really
add	marketing	twenty	charged	matters	reasonable
behalf	mutual	aid	dollar	names	relations
insured	ordered	applications	inprovement	night	route
legal	otherwise	aware	lower	presently	secretarial
referred	toward	carefully	red	publication	session
touch	university	chance	tire	reach	shares
appear	adequate	chapter	useful	response	simple
assured	boys	fast	appointment	shipments	technical
bond	simply	includes	authority	southern	yes
fund	speed	knowledge	begin	talk	young
hotel	ability	larger	contracts	traffic	agencies
located	brought	main	foot	word	comes

140

13th 100   14th 100   15th 100

covers	cities	positions	cooperate	nation	amended
dates	everyone	previously	demonstration	noted	amounts
delivered	firms	principal	departments	proceed	assistant
detailed	leave	profitable	difference	selection	calling
folders	light	reduced	duplicate	specified	closed
inspection	nor	seen	estimated	advantages	confirm
package	often	sizes	expected	arrangement	continuing
paragraph	participate	transfer	finest	associates	easily
pass	payroll	urge	location	colors	eligible
repair	saving	activity	recommendations	consumer	got
scheduled	stand	articles	regional	cotton	gross
specifications	stop	banking	rules	desired	guarantee
union	though	completion	shortly	drainage	heavy
via	trial	congratulations	sugar	election	hospitals
won't	vacation	decide	true	extremely	laboratory
display	capacity	dividend	willing	formal	lists
enjoyed	else	evidence	wire	institutions	minute
jobs	entirely	improve	attendance	interests	processing
loans	experienced	invoices	background	inventory	profits
military	favor	largest	carried	invite	purchasing
modern	industries	models	concern	requires	rent
obtained	itself	operate	contained	satisfied	select
owners	maintain	pipe	decided	seven	shop
passed	minutes	possibility	extension	somewhat	solution
practical	normal	pound	greatest	stocks	studies
printing	opportunities	recommended	institute	temporary	style
properly	prefer	responsible	managers	twelve	table
usually	privilege	society	owner	weight	thinking
worked	territory	agreed	piece	women	trucks
advising	vote	billing	projects	works	warehouse
error	wage	black	rental	chief	advice
film	bad	commitment	tremendous	collect	anxious
fit	cent	death	vice	commerce	arrive
highway	changed	eight	ways	detail	boxes
history	determined	fourth	affairs	duty	clean
improved	east	increasing	beyond	emergency	cross
living	extent	lots	came	export	currently
magazine	front	peace	cancellation	familiar	description
official	furniture	premiums	choice	financing	explained
percentage	gave	proof	cooperative	finish	favorable
pieces	hands	proud	dinner	guide	graduate
produce	helping	regulation	discussion	plastic	growing
reservations	importance	trying	economy	quote	initial
semester	invited	unfortunately	existing	rest	latter
sets	issues	we'll	feature	senate	live
typing	junior	weather	forth	signature	mean
white	length	announced	inches	sound	outline
whole	newspaper	assume	keeping	whose	pays
checked	outside	built	legislation	workers	physical
circumstances	pleasant	collection	moving	agricultural	preparation

16th 100   17th 100   18th 100

16th 100		17th 100		18th 100	
quarterly	limit	legislative	can't	producing	obtaining
reached	mark	moment	caused	reduction	ours
running	mention	nursing	common	repairs	prospective
status	myself	park	contributions	rooms	protect
suggestion	publications	parking	crop	someone	resources
wide	represent	pattern	directed	tests	satisfaction
acceptance	reviewed	permanent	directory	treatment	setting
accidents	sickness	pick	dues	accomplished	standards
alone	sum	presidents	explanation	across	strong
assets	trees	quick	governors	attaching	trained
avenue	yesterday	social	here's	attending	visiting
bonus	ad	specifically	inasmuch	brief	wondering
developments	adjustment	statements	institution	closing	affect
doctors	agriculture	takes	luncheon	considering	allowed
entered	apparently	worthwhile	naturally	definitely	answering
gallon	bid	attorney	outlined	describing	associated
headquarters	carrier	canceled	questionnaire	developing	award
indicates	circular	changing	quotation	distributor	bit
lake	clerk	coast	recall	draft	calendar
library	communication	courtesy	recommendation	earlier	campus
listing	competitive	definite	related	engineers	certificates
load	dividends	delighted	requirement	enter	chair
marked	estimate	equal	reservation	gain	conservation
miles	game	executed	salesmen	I'll	contacted
nice	goes	filled	sometime	installed	corporate
ones	judge	folder	standing	message	efficient
opening	leading	guaranteed	talked	nations	expansion
prepare	losses	lost	talking	priced	failure
provision	map	memorandum	typewriting	refund	highest
rating	mill	merely	winter	registered	instruction
revised	officials	met	answers	registration	intended
started	owned	metal	anticipate	relationship	internal
stay	regardless	natural	avoid	salesman	isn't
administrative	remittance	presentation	beautiful	significant	manufacturer
announcement	safe	pressure	career	spend	master
anyone	serious	quoted	compared	steps	notify
blue	spent	renewal	contractor	tickets	occur
bottom	took	ribbons	degree	uniform	planned
channel	usual	surplus	disabled	uses	quarter
commissioner	you're	tape	employed	wonderful	reporting
contains	afternoon	themselves	exclusive	advanced	represents
farmers	agreements	users	gift	behind	science
fish	approach	wall	gold	bulletins	settlement
haven't	careful	welfare	grateful	carrying	systems
holding	cars	whenever	installation	choose	transaction
homes	compensation	acceptable	joint	executives	vocational
hundred	count	acre	laws	former	we're
impossible	factors	acres	occasion	inquiries	wife
individuals	granted	aluminum	pictures	judgment	yard
key	hoping	attempt	print	notes	accurate

19th 100   20th 100   21st 100

19th 100		20th 100		21st 100	
advisory	patients	trustees	likely	stabilization	southwest
automatic	patterns	billion	music	stamped	square
bags	postal	didn't	necessity	straight	stamp
bankers	purchases	domestic	packed	subjects	statistics
busy	quantities	engineer	preliminary	subsequent	supervisors
ohild	smaller	exception	region	supervision	surface
combined	subscriptions	filling	remaining	tariff	truly
comply	suitable	ink	retirement	thousand	voluntary
counties	surgical	introduced	says	trend	afford
designated	tried	meets	senior	views	applicants
establish	veterans	nine	shortage	wood	appointed
families	we've	normally	shorthand	academic	attractive
merit	wheat	operators	spending	addresses	authorization
nearly	window	option	structure	adjusted	availability
offers	you've	permission	teach	allowance	binders
ordinary	armed	permits	thereof	assembly	brand
preparing	boat	practices	went	assigned	carton
purchaser	bulk	prevent	zone	attach	ceiling
quota	combination	properties	accomplish	became	closely
recognize	conducted	pursuant	acting	communities	communications
relating	dean	raise	bought	comprehensive	containing
roll	difficulty	recognized	builders	critical	controls
secured	disability	rights	candidates	deep	corps
typewriter	drawings	sources	clearly	discussing	creek
unique	drawn	starting	counter	encourage	deduction
vital	enclosures	supplement	countries	exactly	deed
arrival	evaluation	supplied	direction	exceed	delinquent
assignment	examine	tank	economics	expenditures	depend
automatically	feeling	values	electrical	forwarding	efficiency
bushels	fellow	appeal	eliminate	friendly	enclosure
cancel	forces	arranged	entrance	functions	enthusiastic
chest	hundreds	arrived	facility	gallons	essential
coat	knowing	becoming	failed	goal	extensive
consequently	memo	bed	fields	gray	feed
contents	offset	billed	finally	independent	girls
decisions	okay	brings	finished	inside	grades
distributed	paint	comment	gasoline	instance	helped
eastern	parcel	confident	hole	let's	kept
edition	patient	containers	journal	locate	leadership
followed	primarily	deeply	leaders	named	liberty
foundation	primary	desirable	legislature	objectives	municipal
glass	putting	drawing	meal	participating	numerous
happen	qualify	dry	minor	permitted	occurred
improvements	reserves	earned	ownership	qualifications	operator
lead	site	expensive	parents	released	referring
leaving	stands	forty	parties	resulting	replace
markets	stations	grain	party	resume	replying
meantime	summary	grand	reduce	rubber	ribbon
nearest	superintendent	ground	represented	slip	round
none	thoroughly	instruments	retain	son	soil

143

22d 100		23d 100		24th 100	
splendid	railroad	overlooked	lifetime	flow	cloth
tells	rehabilitation	pamphlet	meat	graduates	comfortable
tires	removed	passing	mechanical	happened	concept
tomorrow	sections	plants	obviously	houses	conditioning
undoubtedly	southwestern	policyholders	opened	incurred	constant
wages	speaker	prepaid	partial	installment	contest
wonder	substitute	pump	petition	merchandising	corrected
anywhere	there's	resulted	places	mortgages	costly
applicable	tour	sort	ports	newspapers	counsel
approximate	vehicle	tab	principles	obligations	determining
audit	veteran	text	produced	pair	doesn't
body	watch	transmission	reflect	plate	emphasis
bringing	wholesale	treasurer	regularly	practically	entertainment
brochures	writer	typed	river	prospect	establishment
buildings	attended	unusual	salaries	prospects	fairly
carriers	becomes	wait	sand	readily	gets
commissions	beneficiary	waiting	seminar	rendered	grow
considerably	blind	wildlife	speak	repeat	heart
consumers	businessmen	wrong	stage	representing	heat
continuous	character	absolutely	stating	resale	hoped
couple	client	acquired	successfully	schedules	hot
created	compare	administrator	superior	serial	inflation
discussions	competition	announce	tables	serves	introductory
door	damaged	applying	tools	sometimes	leather
duties	deliver	arriving	whereas	spare	lien
electronic	desks	assumed	wise	star	machinery
enrollment	devoted	bell	additions	stationery	neither
equipped	drilling	boulevard	angle	today's	ordering
examinations	driving	certification	anniversary	ton	ourselves
exhibit	eligibility	chamber	appearance	tool	owe
factor	fifty	corn	applicant	tube	packing
fifteen	forthcoming	disease	asset	twice	panel
hereby	gains	distributors	binder	unpaid	phase
household	hall	driver	binding	variety	pine
illustrated	himself	ending	briefly	accommodations	pink
indicating	instances	engaged	chairs	admission	placing
intend	instructors	expanding	clients	ambulance	prevention
kit	insure	fabric	coffee	amendments	pride
league	interview	finding	confirmation	anticipated	rail
maturity	kinds	fuel	conflict	aspects	recorded
moved	lack	gone	contain	bearing	sessions
notified	lands	helps	contractors	bids	shoes
oak	limits	improving	cooperatives	birth	strongly
organized	locations	incidentally	create	bound	submitting
overall	lumber	inconvenience	credited	buyer	substantially
play	measure	investigation	delayed	camp	supervisor
political	measures	language	easier	cartons	turnover
popular	misunderstanding	largely	employers	causes	yield
priority	neighborhood	layout	expressed	civilian	adding
professor	originally	levels	fixed	classroom	adopted

25th 100   26th 100   27th 100

25th 100		26th 100		27th 100	
ads	team	remind	herein	appeared	population
advertisement	techniques	remove	honored	associate	possibilities
burden	upper	residential	hospitalization	bear	privileges
catalogs	voucher	resolution	impressed	boy	productive
cleaning	win	reverse	imprinted	break	publicity
connected	you'd	rolls	inclusive	buyers	railroads
constructive	accomplishments	salt	injury	cans	rapidly
container	acquainted	seek	inquiring	clerks	reaction
continues	approve	sooner	labels	clubs	receipts
cutting	aside	steam	mortgagees	coal	relief
descriptive	began	ticket	noticed	complaints	reminder
documents	beneficial	timely	passenger	completing	replaced
employer	biggest	treated	pending	conduct	reviewing
enrolled	blanks	valued	poor	confined	rise
entering	bone	visual	possession	contracting	rule
estimates	breakfast	warranty	preferred	credits	seconds
exact	broad	wear	pretty	debt	securities
exclusively	cabinet	wiring	promise	demands	sells
formerly	centers	yellow	proposition	describe	sketch
gulf	circuit	actions	reputation	desires	skills
happens	civic	afraid	responsibilities	difficulties	slightly
height	courts	apparent	role	earth	spirit
honor	demonstrate	bidder	rural	editor	subscribers
index	determination	boards	saves	explains	taxable
informative	downtown	brothers	saw	folks	temperature
interior	drug	brown	secretaries	forget	thereafter
learned	editors	businesses	securing	frequently	tie
leases	endeavor	chances	sewer	gauge	towns
lieu	equally	cleared	shippers	golf	transit
magazines	exist	committees	solicit	holiday	venture
mile	expiration	compliance	sponsors	hopes	wants
milk	fail	computer	streets	human	weighing
navy	flood	concerns	task	influence	whereby
packages	gentlemen	confidential	testing	install	windows
pertaining	guidance	decline	thereby	investments	accepting
pointed	involve	dedication	thorough	iron	accompanied
portfolio	learning	describes	transcript	liberal	achievement
premises	luck	editorial	transferred	lives	addressing
profession	majority	elected	trips	loading	adjacent
proved	middle	enthusiasm	turned	looks	advisable
quotations	obvious	events	typewriters	lose	agrees
rapid	perform	eventually	typical	match	alternate
register	performed	exists	whatsoever	memorial	answered
relatively	plain	famous	wheel	meter	arise
removal	proposals	fishing	absence	missing	art
returns	protected	frankly	accidental	nationally	assurance
ring	raised	furnishing	acknowledgment	objective	auto
skill	recorded	grant	aids	outfit	businessman
spot	reliable	guides	allowing	par	cargo
subdivision	remains	hardware	annum	photo	cast

28th 100		29th 100		30th 100	
cattle	sense	discovered	residents	cuts	specialists
chambers	sites	distribute	respectfully	dealing	statistical
column	solve	divisions	retailers	deliveries	suggesting
commitments	spite	eliminated	rich	despite	supporting
comparison	stockholders	ends	rings	dictation	tentative
contacting	supplying	establishing	routine	dining	tenth
contacts	surely	explaining	scope	displays	thoughtful
contributed	testimony	expressing	seals	districts	tons
controlled	totally	fixture	senator	elect	trailer
corporations	transformer	forest	shoe	eleven	traveling
coupon	treaty	governor	shopping	endowment	trends
daughter	trusting	grounds	showed	equitable	unfortunate
deductible	van	guest	signs	errors	utilize
defective	workmen's	handbook	sponsored	exceptions	vertical
delta	access	headed	sport	exciting	voting
deluxe	accompany	hospitality	starts	expand	withdrawal
drum	achieved	incorporated	strength	forced	worker
duplicating	adjustments	introduction	surveys	foregoing	wouldn't
energy	affected	knows	telling	freedom	writes
extending	aircraft	limitations	thoughtfulness	gained	yearly
flat	airlines	livestock	urgent	grove	accountants
forecast	ample	lowest	utmost	holders	allocated
formula	appraisal	lunch	vary	ideal	appearing
function	arts	mailings	academy	impression	appliance
governments	assuring	manufactured	adjusters	individually	applies
handy	attempting	millions	advises	inflationary	army
label	awards	mills	airport	installations	assuming
ledger	badly	mine	allied	killed	belief
lets	banquet	nationwide	allocation	letting	beneficiaries
medium	beauty	necessarily	amazing	maintained	boats
mountain	beds	nurse	annually	maintaining	bus
movement	bonuses	occurs	apologize	maps	candidate
neglected	branches	operated	assistants	margin	casing
nurses	brands	outlets	assortment	marking	churches
periods	capable	passage	attitude	masters	clerical
pertinent	circulation	physician	awaiting	medicare	colleges
phases	citizen	placement	bag	moisture	comfort
proceeds	clinic	plates	ball	noon	commodity
promotional	complaint	policyholder	block	posted	congressional
propose	concrete	port	booklets	preceding	consistently
protecting	conducting	preference	broken	publishing	constructed
readers	constantly	processed	chart	recognition	conversion
reducing	constitute	promote	circulars	religious	custom
reinsurance	convinced	reaches	coating	requiring	deductions
requisition	damages	recording	comparable	reserved	degrees
restrictions	decrease	recovery	complicated	respective	dependable
rising	deducted	refers	consignee	restraint	depreciation
risks	depending	remarks	conventions	revision	devote
seeking	deposits	reprint	cottage	rug	discontinued
senators	diameter	resident	cream	rush	divided

31st 100		32d 100		33d 100	
drawer	odd	what's	drivers	pairs	transport
effectively	ought	wheels	earn	pension	tree
enjoyable	oversight	widely	economical	philosophy	universities
envelopes	painted	worthy	encouraging	pioneer	unnecessary
equivalent	piano	x-ray	entry	pledge	urged
evaluate	portable	accommodate	everywhere	presence	utility
exempt	prescribed	accompanying	execution	presentations	vast
expedite	probable	acreage	expanded	prints	virtually
experts	promised	advertised	facilitate	promises	visited
fashion	proportion	affecting	fear	proven	walnut
faster	qualities	appliances	feels	pursue	warrant
father	quarters	assembled	finds	push	waste
fewer	ranch	assisting	fort	railway	watershed
foods	raw	attorneys	forum	raises	wherever
franchise	render	auditorium	frame	reasonably	acts
freeze	renew	authorities	garage	receives	advancement
frequent	repaired	aviation	generous	recipient	affiliated
grass	residence	await	gladly	reflects	ages
grocery	retailer	band	graduating	remarkable	airmail
I'd	screen	capitol	gratifying	renewed	announcing
imperative	search	cashier	guaranty	rentals	apartment
import	secondary	casualty	guess	resolve	appreciative
imports	severe	causing	guests	resolved	ballot
incorrect	shortages	cheese	gun	respects	bars
indication	significance	clinics	habitat	restricted	beef
instrument	situations	collections	handsome	routes	blanket
intention	slight	commodities	healthy	royalty	bridge
interim	stimulating	commonwealth	heating	saying	brother
involving	storm	conclusion	hired	servicing	capabilities
lawyers	strictly	confirming	holes	setup	captioned
lies	structures	confusion	imported	sides	carpet
lighting	styled	congratulate	imprint	signatures	carries
looked	styles	conjunction	injuries	sixty	cashiers
loyal	suit	consolidated	intensive	soap	category
manpower	supervisory	constitutional	interstate	solid	charter
marks	suppliers	consumption	inventories	specification	children's
mathematics	supported	content	keeps	split	chosen
mats	taxation	contribute	lading	sporting	clarification
mayor	theory	contributing	lakes	sports	collected
men's	thereto	corner	leaf	standpoint	communicate
merits	tower	corrections	leaves	studying	competent
mineral	transactions	currencies	manuals	surgery	compliments
mistake	trays	currency	meals	surrounding	connections
mother	trim	curriculum	miscellaneous	suspect	consists
multiple	understood	debts	mortgage	taxpayer	credentials
namely	undertaking	demonstrated	motion	tear	defined
newly	underwriting	depends	mutually	technique	destroy
numbered	unemployment	dimensions	notices	titles	differences
observe	vacancies	discharge	ocean	tract	disposal
occasionally	visits	drill	ounce	train	distance

34th 100   35th 100   36th 100

34th 100		35th 100		36th 100	
donation	mesh	wax	costing	medicine	shareholders
drums	movie	weekend	coverages	mining	shelf
economically	occasions	workshop	creating	modest	ships
effects	opens	writers	crude	mowers	solutions
egg	painting	youngsters	dependent	negotiations	sought
encountered	peak	abandoned	deposited	nights	steadily
endorse	played	abilities	diploma	nonprofit	supplemental
examined	pocket	accessories	dispose	objection	sustained
exceptional	pool	accomplishment	draw	oils	talks
exhausted	posts	accurately	effectiveness	opinions	tariffs
expecting	powers	acquaint	efficiently	outlining	technology
explanatory	presume	adopt	elimination	overhead	theater
eye	pricing	advertise	enables	owns	theft
fabrics	probability	adviser	enroll	pacific	thoughts
faith	producers	agreeable	enterprise	packaging	township
fault	proves	alert	existence	partnership	track
figured	publishers	annuity	fare	pasture	transcription
football	quart	aren't	farming	patronage	tubes
fulfill	quarts	arrives	favorably	perfect	tuition
fun	refused	avail	feeding	perfectly	twin
furthermore	remainder	averaged	flight	personality	undertake
happiness	retained	avoided	formation	petroleum	urging
heads	revenues	balances	fortunate	photograph	user
hence	rugs	bar	frank	physicians	verify
hereto	runs	battery	fullest	picked	voltage
I've	satisfy	beach	goals	police	voted
identified	sciences	beans	heretofore	positive	walk
illustrations	screens	bigger	hopeful	preview	width
imposed	seasonal	brick	hunting	principle	women's
indebtedness	seemed	builder	inexpensive	printer	accumulate
informing	settle	bylaws	inserted	processes	achieve
insert	settled	canceling	inspector	produces	aim
intermediate	simplified	charts	instructed	prominent	album
introduce	smooth	chemicals	intellectual	proxy	albums
issuing	solely	chocolate	intent	pumps	allows
jobbers	spaced	clause	investors	punch	alternative
joined	speakers	cleaned	irons	rated	anyway
justify	stories	closer	lapse	reader	apparel
lamp	submission	coding	lawn	realized	appropriation
leg	summons	colored	layoffs	recreation	architect
lender	switch	compiled	leads	recreational	attempted
licenses	taught	complimentary	led	reflected	audience
likewise	temporarily	computing	logical	releases	authorizing
loads	terminal	conferences	mahogany	replacing	bargaining
lubrication	termination	congressman	maker	representation	besides
mandatory	throw	consent	mass	reproduction	bracket
married	undergraduate	constitution	materially	rough	broadcast
matching	utilized	consult	maybe	seeds	brokers
memberships	valve	contemplated	media	separately	catch
mental	warning	convert	medicenter	seventh	categories

148

37th 100

cedar	insofar
chain	installments
characteristics	instruct
charitable	instructor
clothing	issuance
coach	kits
coated	leaflet
concluded	lengths
contemplate	liabilities
conveniently	loose
correction	mat
coupons	meaning
customary	meanwhile
declared	merchants
dedicated	missed
dental	mission
devices	moves
disposition	neighbors
distributing	nevertheless
doors	object
drink	obtainable
eighteen	occupation
employ	openings
employing	opposed
enacted	outlook
encouragement	palletized
engine	pamphlets
equals	photographs
experiences	photos
expression	pickup
extreme	pin
eyes	plane
factual	precision
findings	presents
firmly	prime
fleet	proceeding
frequency	proceedings
friendship	procurement
furnace	progressive
graduation	protective
gratitude	publish
gypsum	raising
holds	ran
hose	ranging
ice	removing
identification	reservoir
ill	resolutions
indemnity	respond
inland	rider
insist	scheduling

38th 100

scholarship	barrels
scientific	bath
scores	beaver
seldom	bequests
selecting	bidders
severely	blocks
shape	blood
sight	booth
silver	bottles
sit	bright
sole	carload
specially	challenge
springs	chemical
stability	circuits
stenographers	citrus
strike	claimed
strive	colorful
subcommittee	columns
subsidiary	commissioners
suggests	competitors
suited	compilation
supplier	conclude
terminate	continuation
tested	contrary
they're	convince
topics	cooperating
tractor	cordial
tray	courtesies
tremendously	criticism
undertaken	dairy
underway	deceased
valid	delays
valley	delegates
volumes	designate
wishing	designation
wool	device
accrual	digest
acknowledged	discontinue
acquire	discounts
adoption	dread
airways	dropping
allowable	duplication
analyze	eggs
announcements	electricity
artists	elements
assignments	elevator
attack	enabling
auditor	evident
automotive	excise
backs	excluded

39th 100

expire	mix
exposure	naval
faced	neglect
falls	newsletter
fan	northwest
fares	notation
featuring	occupational
feeds	officially
fellowship	omitted
finishing	ordinance
fishery	outlet
footwear	overcome
foremost	pack
forgotten	penalty
governmental	personalized
grazing	pollution
greetings	pricer
hardship	proofs
harvest	rapids
hazards	relation
heavier	reproduced
hills	respectively
historical	roads
hotels	rose
huge	routing
identify	satisfactorily
illness	scale
impact	scene
impose	seat
inspect	sensational
investigate	seriously
investigations	sewing
itemized	sharing
judges	sharply
jurisdiction	shift
ladies	shipper
lane	shirt
lawyer	sick
lend	significantly
liquid	signing
love	soft
lowered	specialized
loyalty	speech
managing	sponsor
meaningful	stages
memory	standardization
merger	steady
metals	stencil
metropolitan	stencils
mileage	subscribe

40th 100		41st 100		42d 100	
subscriber	clarify	exemption	jobber	plat	terminated
sufficiently	classification	exhibits	jointly	plenty	textbook
tags	clearance	experiment	justification	posting	thermal
tanks	closes	exterior	keen	poultry	tile
therein	coats	faces	lady	powered	topic
thereon	cold	favored	lay	pressures	totaling
thirteen	collecting	fiber	leader	programmed	totals
tornado	commanding	finances	leased	promoted	toy
tours	communism	fir	lectures	protects	trailers
trading	compete	fires	licensed	ranges	transition
truth	complex	fluid	lights	rank	trucking
unchanged	compliment	folding	limitation	ratio	turning
universal	components	formed	lived	reaching	ultimate
utilization	comptroller	fresh	loaded	rear	unanimously
versus	condensed	frozen	locality	recommending	underwrite
vicinity	consistent	funding	locally	remit	unearned
voters	construct	gate	lock	repay	unemployed
wash	consultant	gather	managed	reprints	vacations
wealth	continually	genuine	manufactures	retention	vessels
worn	converted	gotten	marine	roof	viewer
worry	convey	governing	meters	ruling	visible
abroad	copying	granting	mighty	sanitary	visitors
accumulated	core	grants	mimeographed	scotch	volunteer
actively	counselors	grease	modified	screening	warm
adequately	cubic	grout	moneys	selective	wider
adjust	cultural	handicapped	mothers	semiannual	wind
administrators	cycle	he's	motors	semiannually	withholding
aggressive	dailies	hearings	movers	seventy	won
anytime	dance	heater	nearby	sheep	workbook
arises	dead	heirs	needless	skilled	wrapping
arranging	deals	highways	neutral	slacks	yards
assumption	deans	hire	newest	sponsoring	youth
author	decreased	hiring	nominal	staples	abandonment
automobiles	definition	holder	nomination	statutory	abstract
awarded	democracy	homeless	notification	stocking	accrued
backed	democratic	host	numbering	stored	acquiring
backing	derived	implement	occupied	strategy	acquisition
basin	destination	inability	older	strict	adds
bay	disappointed	inclusion	orange	stronger	adjuster
believes	discover	increasingly	ordinarily	suits	administered
blankets	disturbed	informal	originating	super	admitted
borrowed	ditch	initiated	output	superintendents	affiliation
breakdown	dropped	initiative	overpayment	supplementary	aggregate
brush	elementary	injured	owed	supplements	aims
butter	eliminating	inquire	pace	supreme	alcoholic
button	elsewhere	inquired	packaged	surcharge	alleviate
calculating	emphasize	insuring	patent	surprise	allowances
cap	enjoyment	interruption	payee	swimming	analyzed
celebration	examining	invest	permitting	switches	apartments
century	excessive	involves	petitions	technicians	apologies

43d 100		44th 100		45th 100	
appointments	constructing	fence	necessitate	scattered	varied
apportionment	consulting	fly	ninety	seal	vendor
argument	consuming	forecasts	observed	secret	vendors
assembling	contemplating	fruit	offerings	shade	versatile
assessed	conversations	fuser	outdoor	shirts	victory
assessments	conviction	games	outlines	shoot	violations
asthma	correcting	garden	pan	shops	vitally
auxiliary	correctly	gathering	parent	shorter	voice
averages	corresponding	generated	pen	shorts	waiver
baby's	corrosion	gifts	pencils	simplify	warehousemen
banker	counselor	girl	peoples	slow	wet
banner	courage	grace	plains	smile	wherein
basically	crew	graphic	plaintiff	sod	willingness
bedroom	criminal	guard	plastics	solved	winners
beverages	crops	handles	playing	southeast	wit
birthday	cure	hang	postcards	southeastern	withdrawn
bless	cylinder	hasten	postmaster	specify	wives
bookkeeping	deadline	highlights	preferably	speeches	wording
boom	declined	hit	privacy	stake	yields
born	deduct	honorable	programming	stars	zoning
borrow	deemed	hopefully	projector	statutes	accord
borrowing	deferred	hurry	promoting	stickers	accuracy
boundaries	deficit	husband	pupils	stone	acquaintance
breaker	departure	incentive	puts	strengthen	additionally
breaking	dependents	inconvenienced	rare	stress	adjusting
broader	diamond	inheritance	reactor	subsistence	adolescents
buff	dictating	installing	reads	suppose	adult
bureaus	disappearance	interpretation	receiver	supposed	affords
burner	discharged	invested	reception	surgeons	alive
cabinets	distant	ivory	recheck	tailored	alter
cable	drafts	joining	recruiting	tasks	alternatives
calcium	drills	justice	reduces	tend	ammunition
cane	drugs	kitchen	reductions	tentatively	anybody
captain	durable	lesser	references	testified	appraised
cement	educated	letterhead	refuse	textile	architects
challenges	eliminates	liable	registrar	they'll	arguments
challenging	encouraged	literally	reinstated	tips	arm
cheaper	ended	locating	rejected	towards	arrears
choosing	enforce	lump	relationships	toys	aspect
classifications	escrow	manila	reluctant	transmittal	assemble
cleaner	essentially	mattresses	rely	triplicate	assign
co-op	establishes	measured	remitted	trustee	atmosphere
commensurate	estimating	mechanics	reorder	turns	attachment
communist	everyday	misplaced	repayment	undue	authoritative
concepts	evidenced	mixed	revisions	unitized	axle
conclusive	evidently	moral	revolutionary	unused	begun
confused	excepting	mounted	rewarding	utilities	believed
conservative	exercise	mounting	riding	vacancy	belt
considerations	experiments	mud	roster	valuation	bonding
consisting	fellows	native	saws	valves	boost

46th 100   47th 100   48th 100

46th 100		47th 100		48th 100	
broker	depleted	flanges	managements	prorate	statewide
calculator	designating	foam	meant	prototype	stimulate
camera	designs	fundamental	mechanism	proving	stones
campaigns	desirous	funeral	memos	psychiatric	stops
candy	destruction	galley	merchant	purchasers	straighten
canned	die	gardens	merry	pure	sun
carbons	differ	genuinely	middling	quit	suspended
catastrophe	disappointment	graduated	minds	quoting	sympathetic
chapel	displayed	groves	ministers	radios	sympathy
chemistry	distinctive	grown	mirror	re	tag
circulating	distinguished	hearty	mobilization	realizing	talent
cite	diversion	hereunder	modification	refining	taxed
clay	drain	holdings	motel	refrigerated	taxpayers
clearing	dramatic	hurt	mouth	refunded	telegram
clinical	duly	illustration	movements	regions	telephones
clothes	dungarees	imagination	neighboring	reimbursement	textbooks
collateral	duplicators	imagine	ninth	remained	theme
colleagues	ease	impartial	nominating	remembered	thickness
combine	edge	inadequate	northern	rendering	timber
commencement	educators	inclined	nylon	replacements	timing
committed	eighth	indexed	obligated	replies	totaled
commonly	elections	initiate	occupancy	residency	tough
companion	electronics	inks	operates	resource	transistors
competing	emblem	intelligent	orchestra	retire	treat
composed	endorsed	intentions	orderly	safely	troubles
compressor	endorsements	interchange	organizational	sat	typist
computed	enforcement	interval	orientation	scales	typists
concise	enjoying	introducing	origin	score	ultimately
conditioned	entries	invoiced	overwhelming	secondly	underwriters
conform	examples	joins	packers	seminars	unfair
congressmen	exceeded	judiciary	packets	settlements	unusually
conscientious	exceeding	jury	pallet	sharp	urban
consist	exceeds	justified	parcels	shot	vacuum
constitutes	exceptionally	keys	participants	silicon	validity
consultation	excluding	killing	particulars	simultaneously	vapor
contingent	excuse	kilowatts	partner	sixteen	vehicles
continuously	execute	king	paste	sixth	vessel
coordinating	experiencing	knew	patience	skin	violation
coordination	expert	lamps	performing	slide	ward
copper	explore	lasting	periodic	slips	wardrobe
cordially	extensively	laundry	pianos	soils	we'd
couldn't	faithfully	layoff	placements	somewhere	welcoming
counseling	familiarize	lecture	planted	sons	wholly
dam	farms	lesson	postpaid	speaking	withdraw
danger	favorite	lettering	precinct	specimen	withdrawals
deem	fidelity	licensing	presses	spoke	worlds
defendant	fight	listen	prize	spools	absolute
defer	films	locks	productivity	spouse	accessory
delivering	financially	lodge	projected	spray	achievements
denominations	firing	loved	promotions	stamps	acted

49th 100   50th 100   51st 100

acute	certify	doubled	guidelines	loop	pointing
ad valorem	charity	doubted	guilty	losing	polio
advances	chattel	driven	guy	lovely	populations
adverse	child's	druggist	gymnasium	magnificent	portions
afforded	circle	duplicated	habits	maintains	postcard
afternoons	closest	dwelling	hazard	makers	potentials
amateur	coatings	eager	heading	manage	praise
amortized	coded	electrification	hedge	manuscript	precedence
amounting	collectors	embankment	heels	maple	precisely
animal	commander	emergencies	hereafter	mercury	predict
annuities	commence	enabled	hidden	mere	prepayment
antitrust	commencing	enamel	hill	microphone	presenting
apology	commend	enemy	hitting	midsemester	psychology
appeals	comparing	engage	holidays	mild	publisher
appendix	compressors	ensuing	honest	minerals	punching
appoint	conclusions	entitle	honorary	modernization	pursuing
approaching	confronted	equity	horse	moreover	quiet
aptitude	confusing	erect	horses	mornings	race
architectural	contests	evaluating	hungry	mortgagor	rain
arising	controllers	evenings	hydroelectric	mostly	rangers
arms	convertible	exchanged	idealism	motels	rebate
assemblies	cook	expired	illustrates	negotiated	receivers
assures	cool	expires	impressive	nicely	recipients
attachments	coordinated	extras	inadvertently	nonpayment	redemption
attempts	correspondent	facing	incident	notifying	redwood
authorize	corrugated	factories	incorporation	nuclear	referendum
baby	creates	fairness	independence	observation	relate
balanced	creative	farmer	ingredients	occasional	relates
bales	damaging	farther	inhabitants	occupy	relay
bargain	dangerous	fathers	inspiration	operational	relieved
bearings	dangers	feasibility	insureds	optimistic	reminded
beautifully	daughters	feasible	integrity	optional	repairing
bedrooms	debit	featured	interfere	orthopedic	retaining
beetles	delaying	fifth	interviews	outcome	rock
begins	depreciable	figuring	inviting	overdue	rods
bequest	depression	financed	irrigation	overseas	roofing
billet	depth	flooring	island	pads	rotary
birds	desiring	floors	juvenile	parity	rust
blotters	destroyed	flying	leasing	passengers	sacrifice
bottle	develops	foresight	liaison	peacetime	sailing
brass	dials	forever	libraries	penny	sailings
bridges	died	format	licensees	pens	salvage
brokerage	dies	formulated	lieutenant	percentages	scenic
brushes	disaster	fortunately	lined	permissible	scrap
buys	displaying	fourteen	lining	pertains	seasons
cancer	disposed	fringe	liquidate	phosphate	seats
careers	disregard	fudge	listings	photostat	sellers
caterpillar	ditches	fulfilled	localities	picking	serviced
caught	ditto	giant	lodges	planting	shaft
cease	divinity	golden	log	plumbing	shareholder

70 others

shooting
shut
siding
sized
skiing
slack
smallest
smart
smoothly
solving

spacing
spiritual
spread
sprocket
sprockets
stainless
statute
staying
stenographer
stewardship

stockpile
stream
stricken
strips
structural
subscribing
substitution
suburbs
succeed
succeeding

sudden
supplemented
surfaces
surgeon
surpluses

surrender
swing
symptoms
talents
teeth

tennis
thin
thrown
toe
tooth
tops
tracks
transferring
transfers
tuberculosis

understandable
unions
unloading
upland
urgently
utilizing
vacant
versatility
vigor
votes

walls
washing
watching
waters
weights
whichever
withheld
woman
workmanship
wrap